Endorsements

I've known Cheryl Outten for over 25 years. We first met when she was in a healing group I facilitated, then later as an associate in ministry and a friend. Like many of us, her life has been a mixture of pain and joy. Joy is easy to handle. But, we often struggle with how to support others when they experience the trauma of a life-threatening health diagnosis and/or death. If you have lived through the tragedy of the death of someone you love, this book will help heal the wounds you experienced after your loved one's death. And, if you have not experienced tragedy, this book is a must-read so that you don't make someone's grieving time more painful than it needs to be!

Cheryl Shea, M.Div., RPC, MPCC, CT, TITC-CT
RealLife Counseling Services

This book is necessary since most people don't have the professional training to know what to do or what to say in those awkward moments when attempting to be there for someone who is sick, grieving, or when they have recently lost a loved one. Many say nothing or simply disappear and hope it won't be noticed. Others say things that are less than helpful. Pastor Cheryl's words are validating and, at times, necessarily harsh. *What Not to Say* will help equip you to properly support a loved one and to set healthy boundaries for yourself, should you ever need them.

Dr. Kelli Palfy, registered psychologist
Author of *Men Too: Unspoken Truths about Male Sexual Abuse*

I have known Ms. Outten for 53 years. *What Not to Say* addresses many of society's ingrained blunders and hurtful mistakes, which have become all too common. Our desire to be the hero and all-comforting confidant overshadows the needs of those who are grieving. This book explains why. Using her personal bereavement experience and what people did and said, she highlights why these common mistakes are not only not helpful but are, in fact, harmful. *What Not to Say* will provide valuable insight into being a genuinely supportive and helpful friend to someone who has lost a loved one.

Bruce D. Nickel
Author of the Saga of Eagles and Wolves series

I have known Cheryl and James for more than 25 years. Cheryl has written one of the most honest and direct yet compassionate books I've seen on this difficult subject. I've personally seen the growth in Cheryl's life and ministry. Anybody who talks to someone in grief or despair needs to read *What Not to Say*. I wish I could have read this earlier in my ministry.

Pastor Ray Croker
Former pastor and Cheryl's friend

Cheryl Outten has written a must-read for anyone who has experienced loss. If you are struggling with how to deal with loss and consolation, *What Not to Say*, provides great insight into how advice is received and perceived in our most difficult times. As Cheryl and I met for coffee, I was astonished at what people were saying to her. My father passed away while I was reading *What Not to Say*, and I had similar disheartening experiences.

Kimberly Hayes
Assistant bank branch manager

I have known Cheryl Outten for over 20 years. I have walked with her through the hard times when James passed away. Cheryl has written a timely book. Believers in the Western world need to learn what grief is, how to walk through it, and what to say or not say to bring life to those who have lost a family member, a friend, a career, or one's personal health. The Lord has clearly used Cheryl's trial of grief as a forerunner. She is a gifted prophetic teacher and a true gift to the body of Christ. *What Not to Say* has given me a better perspective on how to respond to the suffering of others. Also, as I read her book, it brought further healing in areas of past grief in my own life and brought me to a place where I could forgive others for the words they spoke. *What Not to Say* has given me greater compassion for those suffering and a clearer biblical perspective on suffering and why bad things happen to good people. If you are a person going through a period of loss and grief, this book is highly recommended for you to read. Forgiveness is a key, and Cheryl walks you through some of this process in her book. *What Not to Say* is a book I believe every believer needs to read.

RJ Galbraith
E-Town Ekklesia, Edmonton, Alberta

What Not to Say

How to Walk With The Wounded

CHERYL BAY

WESTBOW PRESS
A DIVISION OF THOMAS NELSON
& ZONDERVAN

Copyright © 2025 Cheryl Bay.

All rights reserved. No part of this book may be used or reproduced by any means, graphic, electronic, or mechanical, including photocopying, recording, taping or by any information storage retrieval system without the written permission of the author except in the case of brief quotations embodied in critical articles and reviews.

WestBow Press books may be ordered through booksellers or by contacting:

WestBow Press
A Division of Thomas Nelson & Zondervan
1663 Liberty Drive
Bloomington, IN 47403
www.westbowpress.com
844-714-3454

Because of the dynamic nature of the Internet, any web addresses or links contained in this book may have changed since publication and may no longer be valid. The views expressed in this work are solely those of the author and do not necessarily reflect the views of the publisher, and the publisher hereby disclaims any responsibility for them.

Any people depicted in stock imagery provided by Getty Images are models, and such images are being used for illustrative purposes only. Certain stock imagery © Getty Images.

ISBN: 979-8-3850-3926-5 (sc)
ISBN: 979-8-3850-3927-2 (hc)
ISBN: 979-8-3850-3928-9 (e)

Library of Congress Control Number: 2024925738

Print information available on the last page.

WestBow Press rev. date: 02/27/2025

Preface

The compelling desire to write this book came from a dream I had before my world fell apart. I am a Christian, a follower of Jesus Christ. I believe that God is living, loving, and relational. I believe that He is a God who desires to communicate with His children about many things, and sometimes, those things include warnings. My dream was long and detailed. For clarity's sake, let me say that everything has come to pass, with one left to complete: this book.

I saw it written boldly in red at the bottom of the page of a calendar:

Write your book!

You will find the entire dream with the real-life parallels in the epilogue.

This book is for those grieving the loss of a loved one and for those supporting them. This book is for those who know someone less intimately but know them well enough to feel the need to say or do something but are still determining exactly what it is.

This book is for all of us, unfortunately. At some point, we will need it either for ourselves as we travel this rough, unknown yet, well-used road called loss and grief or for someone we know who continually seems to be saying or doing what feels like the wrong thing.

Grief is as timeless as it is predictable, yet it has as many variations as the relationships you hold. It could be the death of your mother, father, husband, wife, child, friend, coworker, or sibling. It could be a career loss, divorce, or some other catastrophe. You will need this book or one like it to help you navigate what to say and what *not* to say. I will speak from my own stories and navigate the terrain I have become far too familiar with, but I will also share experiences others have permitted me to share because they also have truth to tell.

As a Christian for over thirty years, I have been privileged to serve others through pastoral care ministry, prayer ministry, and pastoral counsel. I have loved the broken and wounded. My experience comes from both walking through the valley of the shadow of death on numerous occasions and sitting with those just beginning the chaos of an abused past. I have listened, often in horror, as those before me recalled stories of childhood sexual abuse, domestic abuse, rape, addictions, abortions, and much more.

My intention was not to make the contents of this book feel weighty, condemning, or depressing. It is, nevertheless, a book that deals with difficult and painful issues, which can sometimes feel that way.

I have often cried with those who began to open their hearts and reveal the secrets that lay within them. Sometimes, those memories were released with a torrential flood of emotions that uprooted and told everything. Others were spoken in the smallest of voices, filled with shame, brokenness, and a palpable fear that I would reject them as so many others had. Then, there was everything between those two extremes. I often wondered if I had heard it all, only to be surprised by some more devastating new story.

This book is about what not to say. Yes, you read that correctly. This is a book that I hope will protect the hearts of those dealing with loss. Although, primarily, I will deal with the physical loss of death, I want you to know that these same principles apply to career loss, divorce, miscarriage, adultery, abuses of all kinds, and losing a loved one to the world of addiction. Therefore, the principles I have written about here are valid across the spectrum.

This book is not meant to shame anyone since we have all made mistakes, myself included, when it comes to conversations with those in deep emotional pain. Instead, my intention in writing this book was to let you know that you are not alone in your frustrations with words "spoken at you" that can often feel like a lecture on how to "get better" or to "fix you," all with the unsaid words implying that you are doing it wrong!

At the same time, this book is for those who have no idea how to handle conversations that are more raw and revealing than you bargained for. I understand you. You desperately wanted to help but have often found yourself in a tangle of emotions that left you reeling. You had no idea where to go or what to say to the brokenhearted person in front of you. I hope you will find some ideas of what to do or say that brings them healing rather than more wounding.

I hope you find this book a helpful, healing, and insightful resource as you learn how to walk with the brokenhearted. All stories are used with permission, although names have been omitted or changed for privacy.

James Outten

Introduction

I have been hit with another death. To be honest, I cannot believe it. In two and a half years, I have lost my husband, a brother, my oldest and dearest friend's mom, whom I have known for over forty years, and my father-in-law. Just yesterday, a woman who was much more than merely a friend is the newest addition to the list of losses. She was my spiritual mom! And now, she has passed away as well! This last cut hurts as deeply as the others. Each one of these losses has been felt in a unique and painful way, just as differently and as special as each relationship was. I loved each person individually, personally, and completely within the capacity of our relationship.

I must be honest. I am tired of the fact that I know what grief feels like in my body. I dislike the physical response that my body expresses to the sorrow that I feel. The heaviness I feel in my chest is, unfortunately, easily recognizable, as is the loss of appetite and the lack of desire to do anything. Grief, I am tired of you! I want my life back! Yet even I know that can never fully happen. I will never be who I once was because that person no longer exists.

Grief has a way of permanently changing you in ways that you never expected it would. As it breaks your heart, it also seems to pull the stuffing out of some "puffed up" thinking you might have had. It takes every belief you have and tests it against a harsh reality that you seem so ill-equipped to make it through. It is this experience that has a way of qualifying each of us like no amount of education can.

I want to start by saying that I feel like I am one of the most fortunate and blessed women alive, even though you will find many difficult moments as you listen to my story. While it is true that I have endured many trials and heartbreaks, I have also known an incredible amount of love. I have struggled through the pain of an angry, alcoholic father, childhood sexual abuse, two miscarriages, job losses, and the death of several people close to my heart, to name a few.

Each event brought with it a different type of sorrow. Each one was unique and affected me greatly, changing me from who I was into who I am today. I hope desperately that the person I am today is a better version of the person I would have been without those events. I am, without doubt, more compassionate, loving, and empathetic because of those events.

Let me clarify so you do not misunderstand what I am saying. I am not condoning, approving, or applauding wicked behavior that injures those around them. What I am saying is that those things shaped me. In allowing myself to find help through counseling, group therapy, prayer ministry, and prayer, the door was opened for me to go beyond these events as a healthier person than I would have been had I refused to acknowledge them. The reason I pursued therapy and growth was not to help others. However, it happened when I spent about ten years doing group facilitation for women who had been sexually abused as children. I just wanted to end my pain and rage because of a wounded past.

My heart is tender toward the hurting, and I refuse to believe that a person is doomed to the emotional place they currently find themselves in. You can be free to live, love, and pursue a fulfilling and happy life with memories that no longer painfully take your breath away.

James

I listened to the dishwasher running and the sounds of my daughter-in-law in the kitchen warming up a meal. My oldest son had run to the store for something. I was stunned that the everyday things continued. I needed to eat; the dishes needed to be washed. I thought of the enormous pile of laundry that waited for me. Yes, an awful thing had happened, but nothing stopped. Not one thing stopped. The next day would come with all its usual activities and demands, as would the next and the next and the next one after that. I knew that time would pass and continue to pass until my last breath. I was still in shock.

I should not really be in shock, though. I knew it was coming. I knew he was going to die. I had known for a little over a year that he would die. Yet here I was in absolute brokenness, shattered as I looked at the empty spot on the loveseat that was *his* spot. We purchased the loveseat for us to cuddle up on and watch TV together or talk. He was gone! Really, truly gone! Never again coming in through the back door.

Never again would I be the recipient of the thousands of ways he would show his affection for me. His gentleness would never again take the dishes out of my hand at the end of a long, hard day and lead me to a bubble bath, already drawn, with scented candles and a book just for me, while he finished the kitchen chores. Never again would I find flowers on my table from him or tea beside me as I read because he thought of me as he made one for himself. Never again would I fall asleep holding his hand, and never again would my phone ring and my heart leap as I saw it was him calling.

The doorbell rang. My heart sank as the first of many visitors came bearing food and condolences. Those first people who entered had begun with the usual well-used phrases that often get repeated at a time like this. But it didn't take long to find out that all those who entered my door would not necessarily bring comfort but more shock and horror at the things they said.

With the preliminaries out of the way, the conversation continued in a rather uncomfortable and insensitive manner, "Wow, you look horrible!" I was stunned and wanted to reply with a sarcastic "You think?" I mean, "My God, man, my husband passed away at one o'clock in the morning. I got home at about 4:00 a.m. and didn't really sleep until well after I had gotten home! After spending nine full days and nights in the hospital by his side, sleeping on the chair cots provided, not eating well, and I don't look good! I have lost my husband. My children have lost their father. And I don't look good! What a surprise! I can't imagine why!"

Although I never spoke those words, they ran through my mind with intensity and speed. The words they spoke echoed in my mind after they left, leaving me depleted in the face of my current reality. But as I stood and looked them in the eyes, as tears welled up in my own, I could not utter any sentence, let alone one that would cause biting damage to another. And so it began. Little did I know that this journey would often challenge my character in a million different ways. As many of you already know, some of the most painful things you will have to process are those people say.

There were countless times during the first and second years after the loss of my husband that the conversations and intentions of others left me feeling ashamed—that somehow I was doing "it" wrong! However, I could not stop feeling the way I felt. The pain continued, and the ache of not having James near me persisted. Was I sinking into a world of hopelessness? Were "they" correct? Was I taking the loss too hard? After all, as a believer and a follower of Jesus Christ, I knew that my husband was with Jesus. Shouldn't that make it all better? Maybe I didn't really have the faith I thought I did. Shame.

I hadn't lashed out, although I wanted to. I had watched my husband take his last breath, held his hand, and stroked his forehead as he did it. Death is real. And it is hard! I have friends who have appeared to have handled grief much better than I have, but the reality was, when I sat with them, they really didn't. They had learned to put on a face that would keep others at bay because a smile and the right words make others think you are doing just fine. In listening to them tell their stories, they had quickly tired of unsolicited advice and unnecessary comments. "Why does everyone feel the need to give a remedy?" was a line spoken by a dear friend and widower.

Grieving needs to happen, and it will happen at the pace it happens. This process looks different for each person and varies tremendously because of personalities, relational intimacies, parental love, and much more. After death, we, the grieving, need the most love and support; we need to be embraced and included, not overlooked and advised. Things that are said can make us feel dismissed, dismiss our pain, the loss of the relationship, and the memory and removal of a person we loved as insignificant. Now, I tell people that I was married to James for almost twenty-eight years. We have had two sons together, and we have grandchildren together. He won't be forgotten in three short years. His name must be mentioned. I hope that doesn't make you uncomfortable when we say his name, reminisce, and maybe feel an emotion or two.

As a society, North Americans are ill-equipped to know how to handle the sick, the dying, and their caregivers. The wheels of compassion have (it feels at times) fallen off the bus in many cases. While the bleeding of an open wound continues, so too does the pouring of salt into it. To those reading this book, please think before you speak. Consider the person before you. Look into the eyes of the shattered, see the broken heart within the gaze, and then love them! Pour love into the person by listening; doing; helping; and not giving your advice, uninformed and untested opinions, or remedies! Just love! Just listen! I guarantee they do not want to know how *you* think they should be handling *their* loss.

Let us stop looking at the process of grief as something that needs to be cleaned up and put back in order so that we all feel good and happy again. Death upsets the balance of life! It steals a person from among the living, and you *never* see them again while you walk on this planet! We cannot expect that the pain and tears could be quickly swept under the carpet or taken out like trash. It takes time. I know it is uncomfortable. I know it may feel like it is taking a painstakingly long time—and maybe it is—but it is a journey. Some journeys take longer than others.

You cannot talk someone out of experiencing and feeling their loss or grief without leaving them feeling robbed of what has been removed from them. Doing this will only shut them down and further isolate them. There were many times when I would leave an event angry, hurting, and wishing I would never have to socialize again because of expectations placed on me or comments said to me. Sometimes, it was just so painful that I would come home; sit in my office; or lay on my bed and sob deep, guttural, breath-stealing sobs until the only thing left was a dull ache in my chest.

Moments like this would leave me dreading the subsequent exposure to public gatherings. Preparing to go out began to take on a different reality for me. It included things it never had before as I not only physically got ready but also needed to prepare emotionally, the best I could, for the what-ifs: What if today's gathering brought expectations that I could not fulfill? Could I be happy, bubbly, and joyful? What if the conversation turned (as it often does) to marriage? Could I engage or listen as others complained about their significant other? Would the pain catch in my throat as I watched a couple interact or a grandfather proudly speaking of a grandchild, knowing that would never happen for us? Did I even want to be with other people? Sometimes I felt so vulnerable and would rather isolate and self-protect instead. Each time I went out, I fought a battle in my head and heart as I struggled through the inner questions, *Did I have the emotional and physical strength to handle the words, the remedies, and the expectations of others?*

What I needed most, and what you will need most, as you grieve is to be validated. It is OK that you are emotionally where you are. It is OK that you suffer for love lost, that you cry, that you are sad, that you are having a bad day, and that the joy in the room is too hard to handle. I want you to know that it is OK to be angry; it can be part of grieving. It is also OK to leave an event because you cannot emotionally, physically, or mentally handle it. You are grieving, and the uncomfortable truth is this: you will probably make others around you uncomfortable as you do so. But that is OK too!

If you have someone who is grieving in mind, I would like to gently suggest that you treat them with kindness, love, and respect for as long as it takes. Treat them in the manner you want to be cared for when you are in any kind of emotional pain. If we can begin to pour out the type of love needed in moments of crisis and in the long haul of healing, we will be a much better society for it. Jesus wept; and His heart was moved with compassion when He looked around at the emotionally hurting, sick, and wounded. He is our great example. May our hearts be moved with the same kind of compassion for the hurting because this is the place where healing for others is released and received.

Remember

- Comments on physical appearance are not necessary or helpful.
- Don't give unsolicited advice on how someone else should handle their loss.
- Pour love into the person by listening, doing, and helping in practical ways.
- Grief has a way of permanently changing you in ways you never expected it would.
- Allow that change to happen for yourself or others as you support them.
- The time of grief is when people need the most love and support—when they need to be embraced, included, and not overlooked.

CHAPTER 1

Even in the Diagnosis

The roller-coaster ride began on the day of the diagnosis, and the book *What Not to Say* started the day after. I knew something was coming; I had had a dream fifteen months earlier, and I understood that the Lord was speaking to me about coming events. As a born-again believer and follower of Jesus Christ, I believe He, Father God, is relational and speaks to His children. I have often had dreams that many consider prophetic, as they often foretold events. There would be no way for me to know this information unless He who created me told me. When I dream, I see the colors vividly; I feel, taste, and experience the moments in the dream. God has forewarned me of the death of my mother, father, and husband. Although I am thankful He did so, unfortunately, the grieving for all three was not lessened by the forewarning and still needed to be experienced and walked through.

On September 6, 2015, I woke from a dream that told me something gigantic was coming. Although I didn't fully understand what would happen, I did know it would involve my immediate family and change the course of my life forever. I knew from the dream that whatever was going to happen would happen swiftly and unexpectedly, that there would be hospital stays and exhaustion as I had never felt before in my life. There was also a day that had been circled on a calendar in a month that began with *MA*. On May 25, 2016, my husband began to feel ill.

Initially, he was not alarmed, thinking that he had perhaps gotten a little food poisoning when we went out to celebrate my birthday on the twenty-second. He had no reason to be concerned; he had just had his physical two weeks prior, and there were no problems to report. However, the stomach upset he felt wouldn't let up. After struggling with it for an entire week, he was becoming impatient. As his wife, I was also struggling with my own silent concerns. Thankfully, we woke up to a day of reprieve on Wednesday, June 1, 2016. That thankfulness was short-lived, however. He woke up on Thursday, the next day, with a sore throat that continued to worsen until he could barely swallow by Saturday. I knew in my gut that the dream was upon us.

On that day, I reluctantly went to work. What I had wanted to do was to put him into the car and drive him to our local emergency center so they could begin administering antibiotics. However, I was the supervisor on duty, and that option was unavailable. As the day dragged on, he decided to drive himself to the ER, texting me to let me know he had finally done as I had asked. Unfortunately, the text also stated that he had passed out standing in the triage queue. When I read that line, my blood froze! I looked at those words and a profound numbness flooded my entire body. I knew I needed to leave work as soon as possible.

Passing out might have been one of the best things that happened, although it didn't feel like it at the time. It expedited James's bloodwork process and might have been the very thing that saved his life at that time. Initially, the medical team wasn't sure what they were dealing with; so they did the standard EKG, blood panel, et cetera, to rule out the possibility of a heart attack. I often wonder what would have happened had he not passed out. James had gone to emergency because he had what we believed was strep throat, and that was true. But it was much more critical than that. Again, I wonder what would have happened had they just swabbed his throat and sent him home with antibiotics. What if they hadn't done the bloodwork?

Sometimes, being grateful for the oddest of things is essential.

The bloodwork revealed the chilling and equally incomprehensible news when he was diagnosed with leukemia and sent to the University of Alberta Hospital on June 4, where he would spend the next sixty-six days.

Remedies

I didn't want to attend church the day after discovering my husband was unexpectedly fighting for his life. The truth is, I didn't want to go anywhere. I just wanted to sit with James and drink in every word he spoke, every look on his face, while storing every emotion that came because the doctors had told us the night before that he might not make it past the coming Wednesday, which was only four short days away. His body was full of all the wrong things; he was fully leukemic as well as full of infection, and that is what made the prognosis so grim. The doctors had begun administering two different kinds of antibiotics, saline, Gravol, platelets, and then blood to prepare him for his needed chemotherapy treatments. Within six hours, they had begun treatment. Again, I did not want to go to church.

James and I had discussed the Sunday service. He really wanted me to go, get prayer for us all, and allow myself to be loved; so I went. Our congregation was warm, caring, loving, supportive, and giving. I found myself crying from the moment I walked into the church. It seemed like each person wanted to hug me and pray for us. I must admit that I needed every one of those prayers and hugs! I soaked it all up like a dry sponge and gladly returned all the well-wishes to my ever-optimistic husband.

When I arrived at the hospital, I was surprised when I walked into his room; he seemed to be doing worse than he had just a few short hours before. He was glad I had come. He was pleased that I had brought our oldest son and his wife to spend the afternoon. He was a trooper while continuing to lighten the mood with his sense of humor. It turned out to be a taxing but beautiful afternoon.

When difficulties come, or health issues, illnesses, and diseases befall you or someone you love, many people begin to reach out, offering to help or support you in whatever way they can. As the people began to rally around us, the "remedies" began to come with them. Natural homeopathic remedies, home remedies, oxygen treatments, vitamin cocktails, juicing, vegetarian and vegan diet plans, aromatherapy, books, DVDs, and YouTube sites to visit came in abundance. I have nothing against natural medicine or any of the other things that came our way. I am aware that, at times, they can be viable options. At the time, I was sure that I had heard it all; but as time passed, I stood corrected—there was much more out there.

We found that some remedies needed to be discarded as quickly as they came to us. For example, there is no valid proof that drinking strong green and red tea three times daily will cure leukemia! If it were really that easy, no one would have cancer. This may sound ridiculous, but the suggestion came with copious amounts of both types of tea. I think I can speak for anyone in this situation. Please be considerate when you bring your alternative treatment options to the one who is ill or their caregiver. Remember, they are more than likely on information overload already, and you might only add more stress.

(I will talk about different types of practitioners throughout the book. To clarify and help you understand whom I am referring to, the term *medical doctor* will include everyone in the field of standard medicine, from family doctors, specialized-care physicians, surgeons, oncologists, and many more. When I refer to homeopathic, naturopathic, or alternative practitioners or medicines, I am referring to everyone and everything outside of what we know as conventional medical treatment.)

To begin with, I would like to strongly encourage you not to tell a person with cancer who may be sick and dying that the medical field only wants their money while they kill you with chemotherapy! Yes, this was said to us on more than one occasion. No, it was not helpful. It is important to note that different cancers require different treatments. My husband had no options; had he not started treatment immediately, he would have died within seven days of his diagnosis.

The doctors did not tell him to undergo chemotherapy to suck him into traditional treatments that would kill him. Cancer would have done that. We needed it because there would have been no way to slow the rapidly growing white blood cells. He did not have time to try herbal medicines. Time was not on his side. As I have recently said, I believe in natural medicine and prefer it if and when possible. I see a naturopathic doctor myself, and we have discussed my husband's illness. At the time I wrote this book, she responded that no naturopathic treatment could cure aggressive acute myeloid leukemia (AML). Our conversation ended with her telling me that he would likely have died sooner with naturopathic treatment than with traditional chemotherapy.

One thing that I can say for sure is that your care and concern are always welcome, but please get to know the person who is ill so you can find out what they think and how they feel about their treatment options. Find out if they are open to herbal medicines. If they are unwilling to look into it, your work is finished. Do not try to convince, coerce, or criticize them into thinking they are making the biggest mistake of their lives and that they will surely die without your assistance! People have the right to choose what treatment they want to take. Doctors of herbal medicine and medical doctors have years of schooling behind them. They have a more complete picture of the illness, diagnosis, and treatment than you or I could ever have. Our limited nonmedical understanding of what is happening is expected, so offer a suggestion or two and see what happens. If they are open to hearing about natural health options, please don't overwhelm them with too many facts or data. Remember, it takes a lot of energy to fight physical illness, and the mind of the ill and their caregiver cannot contain all the information. Perhaps the best thing to do is share a little and then give them the name of your homeopathic doctor so they can make an appointment and discuss options if they choose to do so.

Another thing to consider is that patients might need help handling the diligence and time that herbal treatments take. Having my own homeopathic doctor, I am aware that the prescribed medicines should be taken at various times throughout the day, like all other medications. This can be daunting when you are healthy, but when you are ill, it can be utterly overwhelming because you often end up taking many more medications. Juicing can also be a great option, but not all illnesses can handle it. Aggressive leukemias are some of them. Also, preparation is time-consuming and difficult when you are ill, tired, or nauseous. Let's remember the caregiver here. We also get exhausted, and it might not be doable with many other duties to complete in a day. A final point here is that living in Canada in January means finding authentic organic produce to juice is both expensive and almost impossible.

Can They Afford It?

As I sifted through the plethora of books, pamphlets, websites, YouTube channels, and DVDs I had been given, it didn't take long to realize that some of what I was reading seemed to be nothing more than an infomercial or sales pitch. However, some were very valuable resources from which I learned a tremendous amount. Armed with new information, I began to incorporate some into our routine. Unfortunately, much of what I wanted to include was unaffordable because of our financial capabilities. Natural medicine is costly at the best of times, but it can be out of reach if you have cancer. And, to be honest, here in Canada, public healthcare is cheaper. If you find yourself fighting for your life from a terminal diagnosis, these natural medicines can cost you thousands of dollars a month. Canadian healthcare is more affordable. We found that his prescriptions were 80 percent covered by our insurance, and in some cases, because he was terminal, they were fully paid for.

To help you understand the significant difference in cost, I will share an example. I wanted to look at every option available, so I made an appointment with a naturopathic doctor in Edmonton. We discussed several options I had watched and read about in the resources people had given me. We spent some time talking about intravenous vitamin C treatments. We were quickly informed that it is not ideal for aggressive AML and that his veins could no longer tolerate it. However, if he had been able to do so, he would have been required to have at least three treatments a week at an average cost of $700 for each treatment. Consider the price of $8,400 a month for vitamin C treatment alone! That doesn't include additional medicines needed. We would easily have been looking at over $10,000 per month. In my opinion, that is outrageous!

I know you care about your friends and loved ones, but we must also be honest and logical when we look at treatments. We were encouraged by a few individuals to stop chemotherapy treatments and doctor care entirely, turn our sights, and put all our hopes in alternative medicine. I think a fair question would be this: If you find out that you have cancer, would you remove yourself from doctor care and treat yourself with *only* the remedy you are sharing? Would you feel completely comfortable with that choice? If so, that is wonderful. I applaud and support you wholeheartedly! My husband, however, did not. The last question is this: Can you afford the costs long term? Can the person you want to help afford the expense? It may seem like a stumbling block and more than a little unfair, but it is a valid question. Affordability is a huge factor that cannot be overlooked.

There is another thing to consider here. We must remember that herbs and homeopathic medicines are *medicines*. They may interact with other prescriptions, so other health treatments considered must be evaluated by either a homeopathic doctor or your medical doctor before you begin to take them. Failure to do so can lead to a significant injury. My family and I are fortunate that James's oncologist was open to herbal remedies. She would read every label carefully and explain why he could or could not take what had been given to him, and the naturopathic doctor agreed with everything she said. Consider also that some medical doctors will not treat you if you try naturopathic solutions. If you begin trying alternative solutions without supervision or a doctor's knowledge, they can and often will terminate your care. The good news is that many physicians are becoming increasingly more willing to work with a naturopath or homeopath.

Do This Instead

The best thing you can do is listen to your friend or loved one. Hear them out when they speak and ask a few noninvasive questions. If you want them to try alternative medicines, ask if they are comfortable with their treatments and if they are open to looking at other options. Explain to them that the cost of naturopathic therapies can be higher than their existing treatments. If you feel they are willing to get more information, provide it to them. Also, question if they would be open to trying something alternative *if* you gave it to them. Do not assume they would be willing to take something you give them just because they know you love them. However, if they are ready to look at new information or thoughtfully consider the unexplored, ask if they would consider making an appointment with *your* naturopath or homeopath, then provide the contact information of your doctor. Let them know that if they decide to take this route, you would be willing to help in any way, including driving to appointments or helping to subsidize expenses.

Be supportive! I cannot stress this enough. If they are comfortable with their chosen treatment, support them! If they are willing to try alternative medicines, support them. Please support your friend regardless of whether you agree or disagree with their chosen treatment. Why? Because when people are struggling or feeling sick and incapacitated in any way, they need to be surrounded and loved more than they ever have. There will come a time when the conversations surrounding healthcare options come to a close. When that happens, leave the remedies out of your discussions and go for coffee and talk about the kids, grandkids, sports, or some other enjoyable pastime. The reality is this is not your journey. The choices and treatments are not yours to make, agree, or disagree with.

Addressing the Caregiver and Patient

A caregiver is someone who makes someone else's health and well-being their responsibility. Please make no mistake; it can often be as unglamorous as it is selfless. Caregiving will test your limits, patience, and abilities on many levels; but it can be the most fulfilling thing you will ever do. However, it will also cause you to become exhausted and emotionally depleted if you do not take some time for self-care. One of the first things I learned as a caregiver for my husband was that many people had opinions, ideas, and remedies that made me feel inadequate in my role.

As you find yourself inundated by the many herbal remedies that supposedly cure cancer, be patient, kind, and honest. I was not always as upfront as I could have been in many conversations. The biggest reason was that I wasn't sure I could be both upfront and kind simultaneously! There were many moments when I was annoyed by yet another pill and option presented, especially when touted as a "cure-all." I finally got to the point where I asked a friend to be my buffer. I didn't want to hear any more! I don't think I had the emotional capacity to take any more in. It became too much to handle, along with a constant bombardment of information, tests, and visits to and from doctors and nurses.

As I mentioned earlier, it is up to the patient to decide what they want to do for the treatment of their illness. Understanding that they want to live, and that they want more than anything to have a few days where they feel healthy and well once again, should help those of us surrounding them to be good supportive people. Remember that they want to enjoy their lives the way they have in the past but are physically unable to. Certain medications impair memory and cognitive function and slow the patient down, bringing medical tiredness on top of the already-depleted energy caused by their illness. Our health and physical strength are two things that we often take for granted. For those who find they cannot perform tasks as before can often be frustrated with their inability to do so. It is imperative that those who are ill be treated with respect and kindness when they can no longer do certain things, including taking in copious amounts of information and alternative treatment options. If you find yourself overwhelmed with information and struggling to know the right thing to do, imagine how it feels for them!

Caregivers, I know you are tired. But please, firmly stand your ground as you advocate for the person you are assisting. Support the person in your care and love them in the most whole and most expressed ways possible as they maneuver the ups and downs that will come. Do not hide things from them, if possible, and discuss the options you are given in bite-sized pieces to help them understand the information. Then, ask questions that will help you and them come to the best decision for alternative treatments. Just remember this: whatever route you choose, stick with it and believe in it. If you are a Christ follower, *pray*, believing that He can heal.

Please Refrain from Saying "You Are Sick Because"

During this age of computers, human beings have a world of resources at the click of a few keys. Our health needs and inquiries are among many of the questions we can quickly find answers to. Much of this information goes beyond the medical or alternative medical route. Yet, somehow, we feel better knowing that there is a vast array of options at our fingertips. If we are being honest, we know that there have been many times the internet has become our first stop when we feel something "not quite right" in our bodies. Most of us have done this; and then, armed with this information, we head to the nearest health food store or our family physician with an internet-inspired diagnosis. I know that I have done this. For me, it was a successful day when I learned before my doctor's visit that my gallbladder was very unhappy, and all I needed was a change of diet to calm things down. I quickly found that my brilliant self-diagnosis did not impress my doctor, as she explained that there were many other things it could have been that, in my limited expertise, could have caused much damage to my health. Oops!

Our good intentions can cause us to make errors in a less-than-compassionate way while we try to find the perfect solution or reason for somebody else's illness. We want to help! We want our friends to live. We don't want them to suffer, and we want them to be able to return to an everyday life of health and fun as soon as possible, and this can cause the search engines of our computers or phones to work overtime. When we do this, the unspoken question is often to find the *reason* why someone is sick as much as it is to help find a cure.

You Are Sick Because of Sin in Your Life

James and I quickly found out that among the many "internet inspired" searches that came complete with simple treatments, we were given plenty of "spiritual corrections" as well. If my memory serves me well, it was within the first week or two of the diagnosis that some well-meaning person came up to me and told me they had been praying for James. I was thankful! I was grateful to know that there was yet one more person added to the many interceding for my husband regularly. He then went on to add that the Lord had told them that James was sick because he had sin in his life—gross sin, in fact—and that he had not been upfront or honest with me about it.

My response was stunned silence as I looked at him in wide-eyed shock! I don't know what took me more off guard. Was it that he dared to approach me with those words, or was it that I was equally disturbed by the fact that he actually spoke them? I could not believe what I heard. Perhaps it was more the "suggestion" of what that sin might be that caught me most off guard.

We were married for twenty-six years. I was all too aware that my husband was not perfect, but then again, neither was I. However, this statement brought with it much more than the acknowledgment that my husband had fallen short of the invisible mark we aim for in a moral world. I could easily believe he had sin in his life because so did I, and so did the gentlemen standing in front of me. None of us are perfect. None of us are without fault. "And if we say that we have no sin we deceive ourselves" (1 John 1:8 NKJV).

I think I understand where this way of thinking comes from. We are desperate to see a miracle. In fact, the reason you are searching for "reasons" and "solutions" is that you want to see your friend or loved one healed! It is love that leads us to examine the *why*. That one little word unveils many mysteries as we probe in prayer or on the internet to discover why someone might have become sick in the first place. We want them healed and back to normal. I will be bold enough to say that I believe that the North American mindset has become one of finding a solution for every problem so that we can be happy, healthy, wealthy, and wise.

Yet we have countless questions that will forever go without answers! Why do babies die of SIDS? Why do good people have bad things happen to them? Why are some Christian believers killed for their faith while others see miraculous intervention? Why do some intolerant, wicked men and women live a full, prosperous life while others struggle? What I can tell you—and the only thing I can say to you—is this: I am not God. That reason alone means I do not and cannot have all the answers. It also means the same for us all.

If we take the statement "You are sick because you are in sin" at face value, we must also consider what the same message says in reverse. If it is true, it will be true both in reverse as much as it is in the present. If we are to accept that we are sick because we are in sin, then the opposite must also be true: that if we have no sin, we will not be sick. This sounds pretty good unless you are the one who is suffering. Then, the solution becomes very simplistic: if I am sick because I have sinned, all I need to do to be well is to get rid of all the wrongs in my life. Therefore, my healing equals sinlessness, which makes my health about everything I do or don't do. Does it make sense to look at everyone around us, including ourselves, and determine the level of sin that individual has committed by gauging their health issues? Probably not!

You are left with a grave dilemma if you are a Christian. If this is our thought process, what do we do with Jesus? What about mercy, grace, forgiveness, and the blood of Jesus? Christians get cancer and other illnesses for the same reasons every other human gets them. Could one of those reasons be because much of our food has been tampered with: food additives, toxins, preservatives, GMOs— and the list continues? I believe these things must affect the human body that ingests them. However, we must remember that we live in a society where we can eat as healthy as possible and still not be eating food that has not been altered, even if we grow it ourselves.

Have we sinned? Yes! Should we ask the Lord to forgive us? Yes! Just understand that we may be healed, or we may not, but eventually, we will all die. If you are a praying person and someone who feels they hear from the Lord, and you believe you have an insight from Him regarding someone else's sin, please do not beat around the bush when you speak it. If you are going to be bold enough to elude to sin being the root cause, then be confident enough to be specific regarding what sin it is. You may be correct and may not be, but be prepared to receive whatever response you may get.

"You are sick because you are in sin" is not helpful when spoken to the one suffering, the family, or the caregiver for a few reasons, not the least of which is that it could cause a rift in a relationship. If I had accepted at face value and without question what this person had said about James, it would mean that I must question my husband's integrity and fidelity. I cannot stress enough that we are not to throw stones of judgment at any time, but please refrain from it during intense periods of pain and struggle! Ask the Lord to reveal the heart and the sin to the individual who is ill, but be sure you check your heart's motive for why you want to say it.

Statements that come as a reason for suffering do not usually help the afflicted. Instead, it most often brings more harm and pain, including the time during and after the death of a loved one. I remember a friend of mine tearfully sharing how she found herself faced with similar comments when her husband, a pastor, was killed in a motor vehicle accident, leaving her a young widow with two young children under the age of ten. Our words during difficult seasons in the lives of others should be filled with love, care, and gentleness rather than conversations that could be received and felt as criticism or judgments.

Do This Instead: More Acceptable Options

If you are a person of faith, a great option is to approach the individual and let them know that you are praying for them and that you believe that the Lord has given you some insight on how to pray. Then, respectfully let them know that you will continue to pray and fast as you feel directed. This approach enables the one in the thick of it to accept those prayers without condemnation or suspicion that their character is under attack, ensuring they feel loved, appreciated, and cared for by you.

If the feeling to share your insights persists, speak with the pastoral leaders working directly with the afflicted. A seasoned older Christian, such as the lead pastor, deacon, or elder, should be able to help you understand more fully what your role is and guide you on how to proceed. They might suggest that they approach the person in difficulty with your concerns when the time is right or ask you to keep praying and be silent. Pastors also have many connections within the community that could significantly help those in need. Many of them have years of experience behind them and probably have some excellent ideas on presenting your concerns if they need to be brought up at all. Remember, above everything else, when you are with the caregiver or the recently diagnosed individual, *love* them, talk with them about what they want to discuss, and always support them.

A Few Words to the Caregiver and Patient

Misunderstandings in conversations can drive a wedge into relationships that matter or, even worse, destroy them. It is hard to be sick, but it is also hard to be a caregiver. When people allude to sins as root causes of disease, try to listen to what is being said even if it pinches your heart a little or momentarily makes you flush with anger. Take the time to consider if there is any truth in what you hear. What if God is speaking to you through the voice of someone you love or maybe hardly know? What if the words spoken are valid, but you just don't want to hear them? Consider taking a few moments to think about it, but then ask them to come back sometime later when you have dealt with your emotions so you can ask your questions and clarify what they are saying.

I believe if we are going to apply our strength to combating the illness we are facing, then let's go all in. If you accept or agree with what I am saying, research your disease and discover some possible roots. You may find some spiritual reasons, dietary components, or emotional hang-ups that you have been struggling with that may have led to your current situation. If you feel physically strong enough and courageous enough to do so, you may find some helpful discoveries that you can work through. Take note that many alternative medicine practitioners and some physicians will be able to assist you with this. It is important to know that even if you can't afford it, most, if not all, natural healing centers in Mexico, USA, Germany, or elsewhere take a whole-body approach to healing. When James was ill, I called three different centers, and they were all willing to share what they felt might be possible roots of his cancer. When I discussed this with my husband, he received the information and acknowledged it was true because he could recognize it in his life.

Regardless of whether you are willing to pursue this avenue or not, don't let the suggestions given by others keep you annoyed or allow you to become irritated. Instead, give yourself permission to dismiss what isn't important to you and move forward with what is. There were times when my husband would feel the pain of being accused, belittled, or judged, and we would have to pray about it and work on forgiving and letting it go. The truth was, there were many times he was much better at this than I was. As his wife, I wanted his last days to be filled with love, care, and great memories.

I know I don't stand alone when I say my mind can be like a hamster running at full speed on an exercise wheel when something gets stuck in my emotional data bank. It can be so difficult to let things go! I often feel like I am an expert at running a comment, scenario, vocal inflection, or what seems like an unpleasant look from somebody through my mind for days at a time. However, I have learned that if I do this, I must take as much time evaluating my own motives and flaws as I do examining what was said or done to me or to the one I love. Maybe you can relate to this. If you do, you also know that if we refuse to look at ourselves, it can cause us to dwell in a space we should not and come to conclusions that are not true.

It is important to remember that the person who might have just pinched your heart and caused some discomfort probably loves you a lot. Try not to allow your emotions to run wild with out-of-control thoughts that could end long-term relationships. Forgive. Release the pain, the thoughts, and the endless "woulda, shoulda, coulda" conversations in your mind. It won't be easy, but it is doable. This leads me to another area where some people like to speak, even though it is not helpful.

Please Refrain from Saying "The Way You Have Lived"

When we are young and healthy, we often treat our bodies like we will always be both young and healthy. This mindset that comes with youthfulness makes us feel like we are untouchable. We think that bad things will never happen to us. I wonder whether these false beliefs come from our youthful vigor, strength, and ability to bounce back from hardships or if they come from society as portrayed in the film industry. What I do know is that it is untrue, and the way we live our lives and some of the choices we make as young adults often do catch up with us as we age. In my younger years, I became aware of some statistics about commonly indulged-in habits that could bring health issues. Unfortunately, these warnings were mostly ignored by myself and my group of friends.

As a society, we are not so different; therefore, this kind of thinking is widespread. Although not much has changed today, I still don't know many young people who pay attention to the warnings given regarding junk food, drinking, drugs, and the list continues. So when we hear the statistics or read the information on the outcomes of our behavior, we tend to overlook the warnings. I have already mentioned one reason we do this. The second reason is that we enjoy our bad habits and do not want to stop our indulgences. When we enjoy doing something, we tend to look for other statistics that promote, excuse, or put into a better light the behavior we desire to continue, even if it is illegal or harmful.

We know that smoking is one of the leading causes of lung cancer; however, we have all heard how someone's Great-Aunt Thelma smoked two packs a day for sixty years and lived until she was ninety-nine. While this may be true, and she might have defied the odds, she might have had other health issues resulting from her smoking that we are unaware of. Do you smoke to stay thin? I have often heard that line from people. Other everyday bad habits that come with warnings include drinking, drug use, sexual promiscuity, choice of diet, and lack of exercise. Unfortunately, we often ignore the physicians sounding the alarms because we like what we are doing, don't think it will harm us, and often think we can rewind time and bring healthy changes in the future that will prevent these problems.

I cannot deny that it might be true. You may be like Great-Aunt Thelma, but you also may not be that fortunate. You may be able to consume alcohol daily without having adverse health issues or being in a motor vehicle accident, but then again, you may not. Statistics are not proof that your way of life will cause problems for you in the future. Statistics tell a story; however, it is a number, a percentage of people with your type of indulgences who fall into a category you want to avoid. None of us are exempt from the past we have lived. Although we may or may not live long enough to see if we will have any consequences to our youthful indulgences, may this section be a reminder to refrain from commenting to others about how their past lifestyle has contributed to their current situation.

Do This Instead: More Acceptable Options

I had some very dear older friends that I drank coffee with regularly. When the wife began having problems, she scheduled an appointment with her doctor. When it was determined she needed minor surgery, she became very uncomfortable with the upcoming procedure. On the day of the surgery, I called her as she was en route to the hospital to ask how she was doing. She said she was scared and didn't want to go through with it. As I talked and prayed with her, she determined it was best if she wanted to continue her quality of life. She never left the hospital.

The surgery had gone smoothly and without complications, or so they thought. However, later in the evening, things began to go wrong, and a tracheotomy tube needed to be inserted. During the procedure, they crushed everything in her throat as well as caused a bleed in her lung. The length of time she had gone without oxygen before the tube was inserted had left her permanently impaired. Knowing that my friend had been a smoker for many years is essential.

This remarkable woman was like a mother to me and was my go-to for many things. I loved her, relied on her, and listened to her advice as we chatted weekly. Her death would leave a hole in my life like that of my natural mother, even though we were not biologically connected. A few months after her funeral, I had tea with a woman who also knew the lady who had passed, and I explained in detail what had happened to her. I told her that my friend's husband and children were, of course, understandably upset with the medical staff, as was I.

Then, I heard these words, "Well, she did smoke for many years. Maybe her throat was fragile and brittle because of it. The doctors do many tracheotomies, and it is so common. It is unlikely it was their fault."

Although there is nothing wrong with this comment, it would have been better had more information been sought before a conclusion was made. Asking questions helps us get a complete picture of what has happened. When we don't ask questions, it is easy to miss important information; and therefore, we can come to incorrect conclusions. Had these questions been asked, my coffee friend would have known what had happened; and the statement, I am sure, would not have been said.

Although it may be difficult to accept the truth, there are times when doctors make mistakes. There are times when nurses make mistakes. We are human, and human error can and sometimes does kill people. The doctor had called the woman's husband and explained in detail that something had happened during surgery. He took full responsibility for the failure and damage to this man's beloved wife. He was weeping as he apologized for the error that took her life.

Another example would be a family I was helping to walk through the diagnosis and shock of terminal cancer. The gentleman, who had been relatively healthy most of his life, had recently been diagnosed with lung and mouth cancer. He had been to his doctor several times for pain and sores that persisted in his mouth and had been continually prescribed medications, which were not helping. Only after persistent requests for further testing did they discover that he had mouth and lung cancer. The cancer was aggressive, and it quickly began to spread. This man had been a heavy drinker and smoker for many years.

The family was visibly concerned as we discussed this man's diagnosis, treatment options, and possible future. It was only a matter of time before those dreaded words were spoken, but what shocked me was that they came from immediate family. "He had smoked heavily and drank for years, so we shouldn't be surprised at his type of cancer."

The truth that was not mentioned was that this man had worked in construction most of his life, including the demolition and reconstruction of older buildings, where asbestos might have been a factor. Therefore, his cancer may have been because of a combination of lifestyle choices and his trade.

Doctors ask patients many questions as they discuss their health. They consider the whole picture, including how the patient lives, what they do for work, and what health issues they may have inherited from their biological family. We too should be equally as considerate in dealing with those around us. In the two cases I have mentioned above, we recognize that smoking was a potential factor that added to the outcome; but while smoking might have exacerbated the situation, it may not have directly caused it.

We should be slow to jump to conclusions during times of stress. At the end of the day, it doesn't really matter what caused the health issues. What counts and matters most is that the person in need feels loved and supported. How will the past serve the today of a person's illness? Will chastisement for past choices help at this time? After watching several people die of cancer, I firmly believe no one deserves that outcome, and I wouldn't wish it upon anyone.

Do This Instead: More Acceptable Options

What would have been a better approach? Perhaps it would have been not to pass judgment on lifestyle practices. Judging people and making blanket statements are very easy snares to fall into and can often happen because we don't struggle with the same temptations. We can often feel safe in the comments we make if we don't smoke, drink, or do drugs or if we regularly watch our diet and work out. We feel safe because, statistically, our chances of being afflicted with this type of cancer are much smaller.

Comments like these can be hurtful and unnecessary, even if we feel justified in saying them, because of substance abuse and the problems it might have caused in the past. Most family members don't want to see their loved ones suffer, even if they may not have had a warm and loving past with them. I encourage you to work on healing the relationship first before speaking to the cause of the monster of illness or disease at hand.

Remember as well that the individual before you has, most likely, already run through the past decades of warnings and probably wishes they could rewind the time and have a do-over. They know their actions may or may not be returning to haunt them, but our place as friends and family is not to point that out but to help them move forward positively and supportively. Pointing out what they could have done differently will not be encouraging, but it will more than likely annoy them. There is little to be gained by rehashing the past at any time unless it is to bring healing and forgiveness, but rehashing it when you are ill can magnify unhealthy remorse and guilt. Try to focus on what is at hand, the current situation, and move forward from there. If you are a believer in Jesus Christ, pray for them and speak Jesus's life into them. If they are open, help them to pray to release the regrets and sins they know they have committed.

A Few Words to the Caregiver and Patient

I know I have said it before, but patience and tolerance are essential to successfully making your way through the many unwanted conversations you will find yourself having. I understand how this may be hard for some of you to do, but I really do believe that speaking up and saying something as kindly as possible will help you in the long run. Speaking about how you feel, such as what you want, don't want, as well as what you can handle, helps your mind disembark from the hamster wheel of conversations that may get stuck within your mind.

It probably won't feel comfortable or natural, but carefully state the facts as you know them. For example, if the person before you is persistent in telling you that they know what has caused the illness, but your doctor has said that the cause is unknown, gently repeat what you have heard. To the best of your ability, explain what professionals have told you and don't argue. It will likely only leave you frustrated and angry if you try to persuade them otherwise. You can also soften your conversation if they insist on continuing. Reiterate what you know is true, admit that an underlying problem or addiction may have contributed to the current situation but is not necessarily the sole creator of it, and change the subject.

As I round this chapter out, it is important to understand why I believe we sometimes chafe at the comments that come our way. We have unwittingly been dropped into a situation we never desired to experience. It can feel like a nuclear bomb went off in what we had previously experienced in our comfortable lifestyle, and what we want, more than anything, is for someone who "gets us" to come along! What we are looking for is someone who understands or, at the very least, supports us in the war, in the challenges, and in our confusion. Unfortunately, when comments come our way, as well intended as they may be, the words can seem like more eroding of the already-crumbling foundation we are standing on. And this constant tugging and poking removes the ability for us to fully experience the emotions that surface and instead makes us feel like we must shield our hearts and those of our loved ones from insensitivity and the pain of unhelpful conversations. In the process, we can quickly become guarded around others and feel unsafe.

Some comments can complicate our experience, and in doing so, it can seem like every insecurity we had or had not previously known about becomes magnified in the light of the crisis we are facing. In this scenario, our voices can quickly feel silenced as we listen to the responses and critiques of those around us. The comments can make our journey through a very challenging time much more complex to maneuver through because we wonder, "What if they are right?"

Support—what does that feel like for you? What do you need? What are you looking for? Who do you want it from? Support, and what that looks like when you are in crisis, has as many variables as there are individuals in the world. However, I believe there are a few universal truths, some of which are that every person needs to be validated, comforted, and heard. (This goes beyond enduring the difficult times but includes everyday life situations.) However, when you are in the epicenter of a hard time, try to find your support system early. Look for those people who will walk alongside you and your family, supporting, loving, and helping you in any way that you ask of them without making you feel like you are inconveniencing them.

I will mention another thing that may be challenging to accomplish: try to work on positivity throughout your process. Believe in your miracles. Press into prayer, meditation, and daily moments of peace and calm where you can regroup and relax; this will have benefits you will quickly come to appreciate. Work on forgiving! You will get lots of practice with this, so forgive, forgive, forgive. It doesn't matter if you are the caregiver, a family member, or the one needing care; this journey will require things of you that you have never had the opportunity to produce during times of relative ease. Undoubtedly, it can and will be taxing at times. Try not to dwell on the negative things you will hear from doctors, nurses, friends, and so many others. If you are a follower of Christ, I urge you to remember who your God is! Remember what He has done for you! Think about every answered prayer you have ever had and build yourself up in your faith.

Be kind to yourself; this journey is not an easy one, so accept yourself for where you are!

Remember

- Be thankful for the little things; you need all the positivity you can hang on to.
- Don't overload people with natural medicines or home remedies. Instead, ask questions about what they may be willing to look at or try.
- Gently inquire if they can afford alternative medicines.
- If possible, offer financial support.
- The ill have the right to choose their treatment regimen without guilt or shame.
- Only a licensed medical or homeopathic practitioner knows the best treatment.
- The ill are not trying to be difficult, but they are very likely exhausted and on information overload.
- Be supportive—always.
- Do not judge the reason for the sickness or hardship.
- We can never go wrong if we listen, cry with, and love those who are most deeply affected.
- Forgive others.
- Put boundaries around your choices.

CHAPTER 2

Understanding What You are Going Through

I want to tell you that you are doing just fine! You have been handed some complicated work orders, and even if you feel like you are a walking mess without a place to land, you are going through this in the best possible way you can. Good job!

I'm not sure what your current situation is, whether you are in the beginning stages of a life-altering, life-threatening, or terminal diagnosis or have recently had your world fall apart by the crushing loss of a loved one. Regardless, I want to applaud you because you are going through it and doing it the right way for yourself. I encourage you, however, to learn all you can about your circumstances. Like any adventure you go on (yes, this is an adventure, although it may not be one of your choosing), you would not think of taking that hike or moving across the country without doing some research. Most often, others who have gone before you are consulted. You have probably read books, watched shows, and talked to professionals.

Whatever you are going through at this time should be taken with the same care and preparedness.

As you journey, you will learn valuable information that will help, encourage, sustain, and affirm you. Please hold on to these things that build you up. Write them on notes and put them all over your house where you will see them regularly, as well as in places where you cannot help but see them. You may think that this is a ridiculous thing to do, but these notes will help you, and they will encourage you when you need them the most.

Like the pioneers who embarked on a life in a land they had never seen before, you will traverse this unknown landscape and carve your own path in it, which is OK. However, I want to caution you while encouraging you to make sure you continue to walk through and are not settling in the land of self-denial or self-pity, which is easy enough to do. Begin by taking advantage of the resources most readily available to you. Most hospitals have support groups for caregivers and family members, and I suggest you take advantage of them. Hospitals and care facilities also have available counselors on staff as well as support groups for those whose lives have been altered by accidents, disease, or illness. The people you meet in these groups can become lifelong friends or momentary sources of support. The benefits you will find when you take advantage of these services will outweigh the time constraints and vulnerability you may feel at the thought of going. Tremendous healing can come as you sit in a room with others like you, who "get" your pain and struggle.

Support groups offer you a space, a precious environment where you don't need to explain yourself, your choices, or your lack of courage. You are given the freedom to cry and openly share your deepest fears, confusion, anger, and all the other sometimes-chaotic swirls of emotions, which is very helpful. These services are most often nonreligious, although a facilitator will be in the room. You may find this very encouraging, but you may find that you don't agree with everything discussed, which is OK. However, you will find some helpful conversations that help unravel some of your concerns, as well as tools, tips, and resources for the days at hand and those ahead. You will walk out feeling less like you are losing your mind and more like you have been encouraged and lifted up.

Even as I write the words on the pages of this book, I know that it will probably be added information to many others who cover some of the same information, so visit your local library. If you are someone who likes to underline and make notes in the margins, please do so as this will help you quickly find the page or passage you are looking for. Remember, what you are going through is not new to humanity. Like me and many others, you might find your *most helpful resources* online.

Books do not replace the need we have as human beings to be social. So for those of us who are bookworms, regardless of how helpful the information contained in the pages is, they cannot take the place of a hug or voiced validation. Walking alone can seem like the preferred thing to do at times, especially when you find yourself busy with work, caregiving, children, and other family members, not to mention the upkeep of the home and paying of the bills. Also, when you feel like you are not being heard or feel like you are a burden on others, keeping to yourself can feel like a safer option, but I will strongly encourage you not to walk alone. There are many avenues to information and people who understand you and your situation. If that support begins with a book and a box of tissues, I encourage you to start there.

During the struggle with your disease, illness, or any other life-altering events you may be going through, you will find that information can be a solid ally to rest upon. When you are faced with facts, support, and statistics, it does help to settle you in the battle against those who push you in different directions. As a person of faith, this may sound like a contradiction, even though I don't believe it is. I know I have already mentioned the need for faith, prayer, and the trust that God can turn any situation around; and I wholeheartedly believe this. When I speak of facts, I mean it is necessary to know precisely what you are up against so you can understand what to expect.

Facts and statistics help you understand how to converse with those around you.

Having your ducks in a row and your facts in place also helps you to better manage your time, to some degree. Regardless of whether your diagnosis speaks to a long or short-term fight to the solution or conclusion, some things will remain the same through both scenarios. You will find that disappointment and elation often ebb and flow throughout the treatments of the illness. All medications take a toll on the body even though the preferred outcome outweighs the side effects. Chemotherapy, among other drugs, can significantly alter a person's mood. Depression and mood swings seem to hinge upon other things as well, including infections that may be easily contracted, doctor visits and things discussed during the visit, hospital stays, and good and bad days. Vigilance can quickly become hypervigilance when there are so many things to be watchful for. My husband would tire of me asking how he was feeling each day as I watched for signs that would indicate something needed to be attended to. As his caregiver, it was my responsibility to ask.

I needed to know how he was doing, especially if he didn't look well or if he was doing something he shouldn't be doing, like mowing the lawn or pulling things down from the dusty rafters in the garage. (These were things he did while unsupervised.)

We found ourselves sideswiped many times during the fifteen months between his diagnosis and death, plunging or launching us between the highs and lows of emotions. We went into the battle geared up and ready to fight, but we were told a month and a half into his initial diagnosis and after the first round of chemotherapy that the treatments had not worked. We looked at the blood panel page they handed us as we followed along while the doctors explained that James's white blood count and leukemic numbers were still incredibly high. Truth be told, not much had changed according to the facts on that paper. The doctors in the room explained to us both that James would need to endure round two of chemotherapy.

Suddenly, on a day that held the promise and excitement of discharge, we were unexpectedly plunged into a sobering and fearful contemplation of the future. With his aggressive acute myeloid leukemia, the optimal outcome would have been if the first round of chemo had worked. This would have given us an 80 percent survival rate with a bone marrow transplant. However, when that didn't happen, it immediately dropped to a 50 percent survival rate, and we knew we didn't want to hit the next level of only 20 percent. The image of the doctors squeezing into the room en masse with white coats, clipboards, and long faces to explain the bone marrow results will forever be imprinted in my mind.

As the doctors stood in the room, James and I looked at each other in bewilderment. What had they just told us? What did they mean when they said it hadn't worked? Fifty percent? How could this be happening? We had questions—and lots of them. We were reeling with the unwelcome news, and the dread of once again making phone calls we didn't want to make to people who didn't want to hear more bad news was a weighty burden at the time. We had no idea the questions we had after this conversation would only scratch the surface of the many that would come from family, friends, and acquaintances.

When things don't go as planned, everyone wants to know why. I know James and I certainly did. One of the things we wanted to understand was how he could have treatment for six weeks and have so little change. The numbers were almost what they had been upon his admittance a month and a half earlier, and it seemed all that had been accomplished was that the infection had cleared up. How could this happen? This was not the way it was supposed to be!

Human beings have an incredible and insatiable need to have things in our world make sense, and when they don't, we feel the need to create a box for them to fit within. At this juncture, and with the news of the day still ringing in our ears, we had no satisfying answers, only more disturbing questions. What we did know in a chilling and much more distinct way was that James had a very aggressive cancer, and it was difficult to control.

A lack of answers is always difficult to handle, especially when it deals with the life, health, or death of someone we love. Unfortunately, from time to time, that is what life hands us; it happens and probably more often than we would like to admit. It is important to respect those in the medical profession but equally important to keep things in proper perspective. Doctors are not gods, and they do not and cannot have all the answers. As much as we would like them to heal each person they see, that is neither realistic nor should be expected. Many times in the months of James's illness, the appointments or hospital rounds presented more questions than answers. After we were alone together, it was then that we would need to reestablish ourselves, considering the new truth that had been presented.

On the day previously mentioned, we sat in the hospital room on the fifth floor and listened to the doctors. I watched their body language; honestly, it didn't make me feel hopeful. One of the doctors, whom my husband and I affectionately nicknamed Dr. Sad Eyes, looked like she was about to burst into tears! The older oncologist, however, took the bull by the horns and said it like it was, "It didn't work. We will begin chemo round two today. Any questions?"

Although we had so many questions, we could not speak them because of the shock, and the questions we did ask didn't produce satisfying answers. After we were able to utter a few responses to the news, along with a few inquiries, my ever-steady husband changed the direction of the conversation. Being the Canadian man he was, he just wanted to know if he could treat himself to some poutine before he could no longer leave the hospital once again. Finally, a response we wanted to hear! Permission granted! We talked long and hard as we sat a long while in the poutine diner, discussing the unwelcome and altered plan.

Deflated emotionally, we contemplated how the day had begun ripe with the excitement of leaving what felt like prison confinement. We were suddenly forced to trade all that hype and joy for other less positive emotions. It had been a very emotionally taxing day.

I held the phone in my hand and began to relay the information I had been handed. The conversations seemed stale and often empty but not meaningless. Every syllable I spoke made what I said more real than my husband or our family wanted them to be. A state of numbness seemed to be my dwelling place once more. I heard myself repeatedly say, "It had not worked." I continued to say, call after call, that the medical staff didn't know why and that we were left without any satisfying answers.

I spoke, and then I listened, and I tried to answer the questions that came my way. I must admit that some of the questions asked were good ones and ones I had not thought of asking. I decided to write some of them down and ask the doctors the next time I saw them. The truth was, many times during our journey, I was emotionally unable to ask the doctors the questions I had written down because I couldn't handle any more bad news. But there were other days when I had the emotional capacity to do so, and on those days, I asked and wrote answers down so that I remembered what I had been told. Brain fog can be a genuine culprit during times like this, and it would often cloud my thinking. My lack of concentration and recall would make it difficult for me to remember many things, including what I did with the paper where I had written questions or answers. Nevertheless, I did the best I could. So will you.

Please Refrain from Asking Too Many Questions

For those of you supporting the hurting, understand that they may welcome your questions—or they may not. You may think of asking something that they, in their shock and informational overload, had not considered. The things you ask may spark a new level of things they need to know, which can be very helpful. However, when conversing with them, please pay attention to whether they find your questions too much to handle.

A personal example of this came during one of the phone calls I was having after the first round of chemo had not worked. The individual on the line had so many questions I couldn't answer, and I was quickly becoming more than a little conversationally exhausted. I am pretty sure this was coming out in my tone of voice as I was aware that they were becoming annoyed with my inability to give the information they were looking for. I could feel the expectations and what felt like some judgment at my failure to respond adequately. It wasn't until I heard them blurt out, "Well, were you even there?" The words sliced right through me as tears trickled down my cheeks at the impact of those hurtful words. Yes, I assure you, I was there.

Conversations should never come to this during someone else's most arduous hours.

Do This Instead: More Acceptable Options

In my response and lack of knowledge, I wasn't trying to be difficult. I also knew that the person I was speaking to wanted answers as much as I did. I was, however, unprepared for the comment that came my way; and it caused me to end the call rather abruptly, which put further strain on the relationship afterward. It might have been easier to handle if this person had been a close friend or immediate family. All questions from these individuals were welcomed, which helped James and me prepare for the next sitting with the medical staff.

Getting bad news is never easy; medical information, medical talk, and the ability to comprehend what is being said will depend upon a few things. First of all, I found that the level of shock I was in at the time was the primary deciding factor on how much I would retain and how quickly I could ask valuable questions. On the other hand, the doctor you are speaking to is also a significant factor. Please understand that this statement is not said with any malicious intent but from our or my experiences. We found that there were times the doctors seemed rushed during hospital rounds. When this was the case, there appeared to be less time spent with patients, so the ability to break down the answers we needed into bite-sized pieces was not always available. Most of the time, this was not the case, and the staff was more than willing to help us absorb the information and answer all our questions when they had the time to do so.

When speaking to us, a tiny handful of doctors would use medical jargon, leaving us more confused than before we asked the question. Not all doctors had good bedside manners. On the other hand, there were those who were fantastic and very personable. Their wonderful personality and compassion greatly shaped our ability to receive and retain the information.

Make no mistake, we want to hear what is in your heart and the questions you have (most of the time, anyway). But please remember that although we want them, we may be unable to answer them, and it isn't because we don't want to. The struggle is real, and the brain fog is real. Be gracious, knowing that we may not have understood accurately or in summarized form what was said in the initial conversation. There is a difference between hearing what was told by the doctors and digesting that information so that it could be well articulated to those who came with questions. Other reasons for being unable to answer all the questions from well-meaning and concerned people around us could be attributed to stress, feelings of being overwhelmed, and plain old exhaustion.

When we go through the valley of difficulties, frustration abounds! It can and will grab anyone who gives it the opportunity. Those outside the immediate circle, like acquaintances, friends, and extended family, may become frustrated at a lack of answers. But consider, for a moment, the frustration of the immediate family. No person likes to hear this; but sometimes, there really are no answers, or at least none you want. Lashing out and hurting the caregiver, ill, or immediate family can make them less likely to call you for updates. The reason for doing this won't be because they don't love or care for you but because they may be unable to tolerate more pain.

One way of supporting your friend or family member is to ask one or two questions and then pay attention to their emotional state. If they are clear and concise, continue to ask; if they cannot answer, pushing for answers will go nowhere. If this is the case, let them discuss what they want to discuss or let them hang up the phone or leave the room. There will be many overwhelming moments during the journey, and they may be having one. But please pay attention to when they begin to sound or look tired or finished with your line of questioning. When you notice the subtle changes in the tone of their voice, change the topic; let them lead your time together; or, if possible, offer to give them a break from their responsibilities so they can rest.

A Few Words to the Caregiver and Patient

The process you are going through will change you, but rather than avoid it, I encourage you to lean into it as much as possible. What do I mean by leaning into it? Take the time to process what is happening around you, the conversations you are having, and the supportive relationships feeding your spirit. Take time to evaluate your emotional state and whether you are actively avoiding stress by watching too much TV, playing solitaire until it's late, using substances, or any other way you numb your pain. Lean in and feel the emotions as they surface, not so you can stay there and feel sorry for yourself but rather so you can come out healthier on the other side. Now is an excellent time to get to know yourself a little better. But remember to be kind to yourself and encourage yourself. How you handle the adversity you were thrust into will be fine, good, or even exemplary, if you are giving it your all, which I am sure you are. Ask yourself what else can you provide.

As we have just discussed, the amount of information you will get is challenging to hear, read, or digest. Sometimes, you find yourself overwhelmed, afraid, or angry, and it isn't easy to think clearly or rationally in that state. Keep a journal or notebook with you to write down parts of the conversation you have with doctors, some of the questions you have been asked by others, as well as ones that come to you afterward. Take time to process your emotions and then determine if you need answers to the questions you have written down. Take that notebook or journal and put it in a safe place like your purse, backpack, phone notes, or even on the bedside table in the hospital, as I did. Having it in that little drawer while he was admitted allowed both of us to write things down as they came to us. Plus, it was always easily accessible and challenging to lose. After he was released, I put it in my purse, and it stayed there; so when we had doctors' appointments or had nurses mention something, I could jot it down. I found this very helpful and life-saving at times.

If you feel pressured by a well-meaning person, let them know! It's OK to tell them you are tired, overwhelmed, or don't have answers today, and say it as often as needed. Speak as gently as possible and let them know what you need, which may be a little quiet to process the events, appointments, and information swirling around you. Also, let them know that they can write down their questions in your notebook so you can look over them when you are having a better day. I know this will be difficult for some of you—and it sure was for me—but don't let yourself feel like a bad person because you "didn't think of that."

It is always important to let others know that you value their interest in you and your loved one and that you are very thankful they thought of questions you did not have the ability or knowledge to consider. Politely let them know you will get back to them when you can and *if* you get an answer from the doctor. Just be sure to state that there may not be an answer that can be given at this time. Sometimes, in the world of sickness and disease, the answer really is "We don't know. We are waiting to see how they respond to treatment."

If they are a close family member or close friend, another great option is to have them join you during an appointment or two as an outside voice and ear. This way, they can help you gather information and ensure all the bases are covered, which could release some tension and stress. You could also present some ideas on how they can help you process the information given. We were given so many handouts, booklets, and binders that I still haven't read everything they contained. What I needed was someone to read it for me and break down what was contained within those pages in a conversation format. I wish I had thought of this earlier during his illness because this would have been a tremendous help. It also provides your "question-asking friend or family member" a place where they feel like they are a part of the journey. Then, again, it rarely hurts to have a second point of view while reading dry medical information, plus it gives you a much-needed break. Only do this, however, if you feel that it is something you can release or, at the very least, allow someone else to help you manage.

Don't be surprised, though, if you need to cut back on the amount of investment, contact, and emotional output you are expending to the inquirer. If you find yourself emotionally depleted after talking to them or would rather not answer the phone when you feel drained at the sight of the call, you need a break from their questions. So take one! You need to reserve your strength and energy for the fight at hand. You cannot be engaged, alert, and positive to meet your immediate needs if you're drained.

The reality may be that you are fighting for your life or reeling from the loss of a loved one. You may be in the middle of a crisis, a job loss, or some other massive life shift. It is important that you feel like you are navigating it well. It is far too easy to feel like you're not doing a great job, let alone a good one, but consider that you have a lot on your plate. Give yourself some grace; you will not think to ask all the questions all the time, but remember, there are not always answers to your questions.

Please Refrain from Saying "If He Dies"

Yes, you did read that correctly. As you can surmise from reading this far into the book, some pretty bonkers things were said to us; but this one was spoken repeatedly to my husband, our children, and me many times. It was always in the back of our minds, but who wants to put words to this line of thinking? We discovered there were many more people than we had thought who never even considered the impact these words could have on us.

The reality is that regardless of your religious background or belief, most of us accept that there is an afterlife. Many people believe that if they have lived as a good, kind, giving person, they will receive a happy ending where they will continue to live in some type of body in some utopia-like existence. As born-again believers in Jesus Christ, having accepted Him as our Savior by asking for forgiveness for our sins, my husband and I believe that Christians enter heaven after we die, where we will live eternally in the presence of our Lord and Savior for all eternity.

Please note that everyone involved has probably already considered this as an outside chance of happening, but there is a time to remember this and a time not to bring it up. Your circumstances may differ, and you may feel differently about this topic than I did. I didn't want to dwell on this thought. It wasn't until the bitter end, when I could see his body was beginning to shut down, that I realized, short of a miracle, he didn't have long to live. It was only then that I could start to wrap my head around what would happen if he died. You see, I didn't want to think of this kind of separation from the man I loved, regardless of how good it would be for him!

The reality of this comment hit me hard as I entered the church after the second hit when we found out the chemotherapy had not worked. Knowing we were down to a 50 percent survival rate was like a constant ringing in my ears that I could not stop. When I entered the door into the sanctuary of my home church, I was met with the statement, "Well, if he dies, at least you know where he will be going. That's got to help!" I burst into tears.

No! It did not help! I was distraught! I was upset with the truth that my husband was still in the hospital and that the weekend we had planned with the family would not be taking place anytime soon. I was upset that his chances of survival had diminished, that he would be sick with treatment again, and that the never-ending trips to the University of Alberta Hospital would continue. I was upset because he was ill. I was upset because we were not together. I was upset because my kids were upset. I was upset because his mother sobbed so hard on the phone, and his dad got angry when he heard the news. No, that thought did not help.

I couldn't stop the tears from raining down my cheeks because I understood that this comment was meant to bring encouragement to me—but it didn't. I may be the only one out there, but somehow, I don't believe I am, but this statement angered me! At that time, it felt so insincere, like a passive cliché that we speak when we feel the need to say something to soothe the emotional pain. It shut the door on James's, my kids', and his parents' feelings. It closed the door on my feelings and anything I would want to say. It silenced us because, of course, we shouldn't feel bad for him, even though he was suffering now and we were afraid that he would die!

You may not have thought of this until this moment, but this statement takes away so much from the ones who love those who are critically ill as well as from the ones who are caring for them. There is something very remarkable in knowing that a person will spend eternity with Jesus, and it does us good to think about this often. I also believe we should remember that Jesus never once overlooked a person for how they felt! He validated people in their grief and pain and did not dismiss their emotions with a comment. Jesus had a heart of compassion for the crowd. It moved His heart to meet them in their need: heal them, hear them, and touch them. He was personal, and he showed empathy.

"Well, if he dies, at least you know where he will be going! That's got to help!" I remind you of what was said because this statement had come on the heels of devastating news and did nothing for those of us suffering. The reality that you cannot see and know nothing about is that a quick five-second statement could be preceded by thousands of moments of heartache, so please don't dismiss that. I was the one who looked into the eyes of my oldest son. When I explained to him the reality of the situation, I saw the devastation on his face. I heard the pain in my youngest son's voice and was aware of its cracking as emotion welled up while he tried to hold it together over the phone. I sat quietly on the phone as my mother-in-law wept, and I heard the door slam as my father-in-law left the house. We were hurting, we were aching inside and emotionally fragile, and I felt very insecure at that time. What we needed was time to be where we were and settle this horrible information individually and as a family. While he was still living, we did not need to be told that his death would be a grand celebration.

Do This Instead: More Acceptable Options

You have a good heart, and you are a good person, and I also know you love your friend(s). I understand that your intentions are meant to bring comfort, and for some, comments about heaven might do that. But may I suggest that instead of going to death as the final outcome in the initial stages of a diagnosis like this, you hang on to life, hope, and faith. Continue to believe that healing may happen and that remission, stem cell transplant, surgery, or whatever other options there might be are definite possibilities. Keep those thoughts of death to yourself. Most of all, listen! To be completely honest, there seemed to be a very fine line between the statements about the "heavenly celebration" and those that continually came back around to total healing as the only things people focused on. He was still alive! If you are at a loss at what to do in a moment like this, prayer is usually safe as long as you don't dismiss their messy emotional state or expect a hearty hallelujah or a complete turnaround in their feelings. Pray for strength, hope, courage, and healing; however, please stay away from preaching to them while you pray. They need love! Just love and huge doses of understanding.

Other ways you can help during peak moments of trouble is to invite the person or family to dinner or offer to bring a cooked meal to their home. Spending time with those hospitalized or at home when discharged is always welcome and is much more uplifting than you know. Sick people need company! They need to know they matter and that people care about them. The only thing that has changed for them is that they got sick, maybe even terminally ill, but they will still enjoy having a good laugh and an inspiring visit. Having regular days with friends who can get them into hearty conversations, complete with belly laughs, is imperative to help them take a break from the issues that seem to be constantly in front of them. Take the opportunity to let them know that you are thinking and praying for them and that you understand that this is a difficult time for everyone involved.

Suppose your schedule or lifestyle doesn't allow you the ability to be there in person. In that case, gift cards for restaurants, coffee, or gas cards are also very thoughtful and greatly appreciated gestures. Today, I am still so thankful for all these gestures supplied to me and my family during the hospital stays. It made such a massive difference in so many ways, and it did help us to know we were being thought of and cared for.

If you don't know what to say at the time you hear bad news or think you might be weird and awkward in front of the hurting, I will tell you this: very often, the most meaningful things said were admissions from the person in front of me that they didn't know what to say. Those who were honest enough to say that they were sorry that things went the way they did but also wished there was something they could do to change it touched me deeply. It was like they were looking into my eyes, or the eyes of my family members, as we suffered and then jumped in the boat and grabbed an oar to help lighten the load. Never be afraid to say you don't understand and have no idea how to respond because there is something very comforting in hearing someone say that they are feeling as helpless as you are.

I want to elaborate on a point I made earlier. Spending time with those enduring difficulty and their caregivers is life-giving! When bad news rears its ugly head, and hopes are crushed, a visit and some laughter may be vital to help improve the family's overall emotional and mental health. What tends to happen, and what did happen in our journey, was that most people waited until the last days of his life to show up with Timmy's coffee and a short visit. The thing to remember is that they need you now! They need to know that they are not walking alone. Spend as much time with them as you can while you can. This selfless gesture is not one you will regret! Yes, be time-conscious because they may find a long visit strenuous and exhausting, but please come for a visit. I have heard from far too many people that this was the case for them as well. We need to show up, not just talk about it.

My husband enjoyed the visits with friends when they came, and I can attest that they didn't come often enough. He spent far too many days alone with only his mind, his illness, and the beeping of machines to occupy his thoughts. We are made to live in community. If we feel like we are removed from it, our mental health will suffer, not to mention that we often feel worse physically when all we have to do is focus on ourselves. Show up for them! Go for a walk if they can, take them for coffee, or bring coffee, a snack, or lunch. The emotional uplift will bring them so much joy.

A Few Words to the Caregiver and Patient

As a caregiver, I found that occasional solitude was a wonderful reprieve. I was still working at the bank, and between dealing with the challenges of my job and traveling into the city to see James after work, I could feel the stress building up within me. When I needed to recharge, I would go home, draw a bubble bath, and soak as long as I wanted to while listening to some good worship music. No guilt allowed!

Another thing I would do to help myself unwind was pray while I drove into the city. This may not be for everyone, and I understand that; but as a believer in Christ, it helped me dump my stress onto someone more significant and more able, and one I believe has all the answers. I could be loud, quiet, contemplative, and completely raw and honest. I would present all my concerns from the day at work and the upcoming visit with my husband and ask the Lord to help me be prepared for any unwelcome doctor visits or notes on his chart. I held nothing back when talking to Him; so if tears were my mode of expression on any given day, then that is what I did, knowing He would accept me as I was.

However, for my husband and me, there was something very soul-soothing sitting with a friend and laughing and talking about something other than the beast we were facing. When that is what you need, call up a friend and ask if you can go for a midafternoon coffee or take a break from making dinner and go out to eat a good meal as a diversion. I give you permission to have a few moments to enjoy yourself during the stress.

For those of you most directly affected by what is happening, the patient, I am addressing you now. Please don't wait until someone decides to come and visit you because the unwelcome truth is they may not. Please understand that it probably won't be because they don't want to but rather because most people are uncomfortable around the unknown. Unfortunately, at the moment, you fit into that category and within the framework of that internal struggle they might be facing. You know who your friends are, so call and talk to them over the phone and let them know you would love to see their faces. A one-on-one visit would be lovely. While you are at it, ask them to bring you your favorite treat, a book, or something else you enjoy doing. A young woman who wasn't sure what to do would buy small *Star Wars* Lego sets for James to put together, and he absolutely loved that. It brought him so much joy! So please don't be shy; find out from them what they could and would be willing to bring you. Let them know that sitting at home or in the hospital is boring and seems worse when you are not feeling well. Most people want to do something for you, so let them! Make a list and then begin to make your requests known, but above all, be honest. If it is important to you to have visitors, make sure you say that, but remember that even phone visits are better than nothing. If you are mobile and can get out, you call and make plans, but do not sit alone and let your mind wander into unhealthy territory. I permit you to get your needs met.

Please Refrain from Assuming

As humans, we have some common struggles. Sometimes, we get ill and don't recover, even when we access all modalities. As believers, prayer is one of those things we can give our all to; and yet, sometimes, it comes up without the resolve we seek. This can be one of the hardest things to deal with. In fact, when you are doing everything you know to do, have been told to do, and are diligent in doing, you expect results, right? I feel like one of the reasons it is so difficult to handle is because of the cyclical pattern of illnesses that we are most familiar with. For example, we get ill with the flu, and we recover. We get an infection or injury, and we recover over time. Sure, there may be the need to endure the inconvenience of a cast for a short time, be on antibiotics, or stay home from work; but we know that, most often, if we follow the usual protocol, we will rather quickly put it entirely behind us.

Also, from time to time, when we are well, we may listen to stories of those who beat the odds of poverty, illness, or death. These inspirational stories often give us hope and help us feel prepared on how we can get a positive outcome if and when we get hit with something similar. However, this can also create a mindset in some that is akin to people who have advice for things they have no experience in, much like adults with no children giving parenting advice to those who do. It just doesn't work, and it is not helpful in any way. When we are on the outside looking in, it is easy to feel like we have answers to questions we have not been asked and to problems we are not faced with.

On one occasion, while I was in church, as I stood up to gather my things from the chair beside me to move on with my busy day, I made eye contact with a woman standing behind me. Without saying a word, she passed me a CD. The look on her face was one I would never forget, as it cut right through me. As I looked down at the CD, I saw the words *Healing Scriptures* across the disk. The message I got was that I should know better. I was doing it wrong!

I must confess that I was getting worn out at this point in the months of emotional pain and many disappointments. I needed to learn to dodge unwanted comments and judgmental, critical, and non-supportive people and conversations for my own mental and emotional well-being. I blurted out, "What is this?" Her response was "Well, you know. Listen to it all day long, even while you're sleeping, and he will be healed!" I turned and walked away, CD in hand, with my temper barely controlled.

Why hadn't I thought of that? I mean, if all we needed to do is listen to the CD all day and night while drinking copious amounts of green and red tea, anoint him with oil, do communion together daily, read and pray the scriptures daily, cut out all sugar, stop medical treatment, eat no meat, consume no dairy, take the right supplements, and just believe and have faith, the healing would be a done deal! Sounds so easy. Good grief! I can laugh now as I reflect on that day, but at the time, it was not funny or helpful.

Do This Instead: More Acceptable Options

I appreciate the gesture and recognize it was intended to be kind. I acknowledge that it took time to gather the scriptures and burn the CD, and the thought that went into making it was lovely. As I look back on it, it had more to do with the delivery of the gift. It would have been nice if she had at least conversed with me rather than silently thrusting it toward me in an abrupt and final manner. Once again, I want to mention that when life-altering events occur, every possible emotional and mental resource you have is in high demand for those going through it. It doesn't take long before your emotional and spiritual tanks get low and drain in time. Filling them up again can be challenging when so much time and energy are being spent in more depleting ways. Time is not always available to do so because you can often be pulled in many different directions.

What did I want in the conversation that didn't happen? I think it would have been helpful for her to have let me know that she had thought of us and was wondering if we had already considered listening to healing scriptures in the background as we went through our day. Unfortunately, she didn't know that we had already adopted this into our routine, but I didn't have the capacity to tell her that on that day.

Attitude is everything, especially in a situation like this. Be personable and always be as loving as possible. When we understand that any gesture can be received or rejected based on how it comes across, even during life-giving and delightful times, it should help us to be more sensitive. Many times, it isn't what you say or do but *how* you say or do it! In the above scenario, it wasn't the gift but the presentation that was off. Had they let me know that they had been praying and had personally gathered the scriptures for my husband and the rest of us as his family, it could have led to a delightful conversation. Honestly, at the time, just the thought of taking the time to do one more thing in the day felt like the straw that would break the camel's back. Acute myeloid leukemia has many demands; and sometimes, the silence at the end of the day, or anytime during the day, is truly golden.

Assumptions are never helpful and are usually inaccurate. Your gifts and gestures will likely be received with heartfelt appreciation, but I suggest you ask if they are open to what you are presenting. Have a conversation, find out what they are doing, and try to come alongside that; but as believers in a God who heals, do not assume they are not healed because they are not tapping into your desired resources. He is the source who heals.

A Few Words to the Caregiver and Patient

The event above may never happen to you, but it might. If it does, I pray that it comes across with the love and thoughtfulness that the gift giver intended. You can be gracious and respectful as you take the gift but don't feel it carries the magic potion to change your situation. Don't add more pressure on yourself. Only do as requested if it makes sense to you if you have time to do it, and if you want to. Your first priority is managing your time, energy, work, family, and everything else you must do. Adding more to do because you want to accommodate others and their suggestions won't make you feel any better in the long run; it may only make you feel bitter, and we don't want to go there.

There is nothing wrong with taking every kind gesture shown to you as something worthy of consideration because it just might be. On the other hand, give yourself the right to let yourself off the hook if you are already doing something similar or don't feel like you can manage one more thing on your plate. My husband and I built up our Christian faith; we watched the right programs on TV, read books on healing, listened to testimonies of those who were healed, and absorbed the Word of God. We stepped out in faith, made long-term plans and goals for holidays, and renewed his passport for ten years. We discussed renovating the house and looked at what yard upgrades we liked and could afford. We also discussed church and ministry, family, our upcoming grandchildren, and much more as we exercised our faith to help us believe and prepare for complete healing and restoration. We had the pastor and the elders come and pray, we anointed with oil and had communion with them, we repented and made proper confessions where needed. We believed. We had faith.

As I mentioned before, perhaps if the CD giver and I had had an actual conversation, it would have allowed these pieces of information to come out and helped us both find a sense of greater peace in our hearts and relationship rather than the distance it did bring. One of the things I have learned through the years is to be as kind as possible while being as honest as I should be. Doing this helps me maneuver a problematic or uncomfortable situation with integrity and love. At the same time, it also allows a further conversation to occur if my honesty or theirs wasn't well received. One of the best things you can do for yourself in these moments is to remove pressure, stress, and expectations from your life as opposed to adding more to the pile.

The second round of chemotherapy and subsequent bad news came with what felt like a tsunami wave as the news sank in that we were in for the long haul, with an increased possibility of an unwelcome end. We entered the arena where no information seemed to be good news, but friends and acquaintances began to rally around us. We felt the love and support of many of those people and were encouraged by the many texts and well-wishes we received from them. James and I came into the circle of believers and decided to "stay positive and stay in faith," and we all doubled down on our prayers for him. He had walked through the first round of chemo so well that we expected the second to be much the same. It wasn't.

Now that I look back on it, perhaps we should have realized the first round wasn't working because he didn't seem to have any side effects. He was so ill when he went into the hospital with an infection and significantly elevated white blood cell counts that we were unsure what was taking the worst toll on him. As it turns out, within the week, as soon as he started to recover from the infection, he perked right up and became his usual self. His skin turned slightly yellow, and he was tired, but that was all the side effects he had. At the time, we found this very encouraging news, thinking that the prayers were working. We thanked God for none of the nasty side effects that often come with chemotherapy.

After the first round of treatments was done, James completed his second bone marrow test. A very somber doctor handed us the blood test results. "It didn't work. It didn't really do much, to be honest," she informed us. We were shaken to the core. This was not what we were expecting to hear! We both wanted explanations! James felt well. He looked well and seemed to be fine in every respect. Except he wasn't.

Blasted leukemia, anyway! How can cancer be killing a person without them even knowing it? How is it possible that a man is living his life without any indication that his blood is killing him? How was it possible that we were a month in on this journey, feeling optimistic that things were going well with few indications that anything was wrong, only to find out that things were still very, very bad! I find it difficult to describe how mentally debilitating it was to know that my husband was still a very ill man. It took the wind out of our sails to discover that we would be separated for another month. We were not only upset but also deflated. Suddenly, we felt more than a little scared.

What do you do in this situation? What do you do when life continues to throw you curveballs? You journey on. You journey on because you cannot stay in the moment. You cannot rewind time. As much as you want to hang on to today, the moments will pass, the day will end, and you will have to face tomorrow. That is what we did. We kept putting one foot in front of the other, not because we wanted to but because that was the only choice afforded to us. One day turned into the next and the next and the next. Time didn't stand still, and so we decided to become engaged in the process he was on. We needed to be as involved as possible with what was happening with the current diagnosis and what that meant for him and his treatment, his lifespan, and his emotional, physical, and mental well-being.

At that moment with the doctor, in that room with my husband, with the blood results page in my shaking hand, I was thinking of none of those things. Instead, I was reminding myself to breathe in and out. I was trying very hard to get the ringing in my ears to quiet so that I could hear the doctor's words and maybe comprehend a sentence or two. Some things changed that day, while others stayed much the same. I noticed immediately that my introverted husband, as always, became even more introspective and quiet. That was true to who he was when he was working through something, and he needed to settle the information in his heart and process his thoughts and questions. I, however, went home and cried.

Please Refrain from Telling "the Stories"

Everyone loves a good story, especially if it has a happy ending! It is one of the reasons we go to the movies and theaters and read books. We like to hear of the daring feats of those who have climbed the highest mountains or overcome the most significant obstacles, and it is because of this that real-life stories are so popular. *Apollo 13* and *Titanic*, among others, were not box-office hits because we didn't know what would happen. No, it was because we did. These movies put a personal spin on an event that caught our attention in a heartfelt way that caused our emotions to choke in our throats and run down our faces.

It was during the second round of treatment that the stories really began to flood in. We had heard a few before this, but as people rallied with hope in their hearts to encourage James to live, we suddenly found ourselves immersed in them. Stories of hope, survival, and many stories of miracles seemed to be on the lips of what seemed like almost every person we met. I quickly noticed, however, that the stories I heard most often seemed to come from a third party. Whatever way a tale is told is acceptable; I have no problem with that. But it would have been nice to have coffee with a few of the healed overcomers themselves, you know, so we could ask some questions and hear their firsthand encounter with the difficulties and opposition they faced. However, precisely as these testimonies were meant to do, they brought us hope and encouragement and built us up to believe in survival and the return to total health.

There is a time to do this and a time to refrain from it. As Ecclesiastes says, "There is a season for everything under the sun." It was a tremendous help to hear those stories during the first and second rounds of treatment, but toward the end of the fifteen months of his fight, they became like the sound of fingernails on a chalkboard. I wish I could say that the only stories ever told to us were those that lifted us emotionally and spiritually, but unfortunately, that was not the case. There are many people out there who want to tell their painful stories to relate to your situation. So if you are interested in telling your tale so you can launch into your personal stories of unexpected and horrific illnesses and shocking death details, please don't do it! Now is not the time.

When my husband and I began our phone calling and text messaging to relay the unwelcome news that he was still a very sick man, I found myself confronted with some of these unpleasant info bites. "It is just like my husband's cancer," as the woman on the other end of the phone began to recite, in detail, the list of horrific events of her husband's prolonged cancer. I began to shrink inside. I had known the man. He had died. The only thing I knew as I listened to her rattle on was that this was not what I needed to hear at this particular moment. I should have said something then but didn't. As I continued to listen to her story unfold, I was led to believe that from beginning to end, it was entirely the fault of the doctors that he did not live. According to her telling of the events, all the doctors who had been treating her spouse were utterly inept in their profession. With one mistake after another, he had died a horrific death; and unfortunately, as she recited the details, she put James and me on the same unwanted track. It felt like I was given an unwelcome invitation to a club I didn't care to join.

I wanted to shout, "This isn't about you. This is not helping. STOP TALKING!" I was too polite for that, however. Instead, I tried to get off the phone but could not do so because of the relentless stream of words that filled up every second on the phone. I don't know how long we were into the call when I forcefully blurted out that I couldn't talk to her and hung up the phone. I never directly called her again, although I did keep her in the loop through another source. It's true; I did have other phone calls to make, but I needed support, not an unhealthy and bitter monologue.

Women, we do this all the time. Think about your last interaction with the new first-time expectant mother and consider your conversation and those of the others around you. We ask them questions about how they are feeling. Are they nauseous? Do they have morning sickness? How are they sleeping? Then, we often launch into filling the gaps in conversation with our own pregnancy experiences, birthing stories, and all things prenatal. We tend to do the same thing after the baby is born. Consider the baby shower, ladies. Why is it that we ask questions at this time? Are we asking to listen for the answers, or so we can share about ourselves?

The newly pregnant, first-time mom doesn't want to hear about your pregnancy and birthing story. She wants to tell her own. It is her time to shine. The moment is hers; let her enjoy it. She also doesn't need to have an anxiety attack because you had a rough go of it, and now your voice is trapped in her head. As you keep this in mind, there is a good chance that the person in the middle of the cancer battle also doesn't want to hear about your uncle's twenty-year struggle with prostate cancer, either. It wasn't that we didn't care, but we didn't want to hear about the childhood friend who had battled leukemia three times and survived all three battles without a stem cell transplant before he was twenty-five. We were glad he was doing great, but the cancers were vastly different, even though they both bear the name leukemia.

Even if what is being said is positive in nature, it can still minimize the experience, struggle, and pain of the person in front of you. Not all cancers are the same, not all treatments are the same, and therefore, not all the outcomes are the same. Please, don't make their struggle about you or someone you know. Although you mean well, the retelling of your events can cause those at the center of the issue to begin to shut down or compartmentalize in an unhealthy way. If you think they may benefit from something you have gone through, ask if you can share it with them and guard against being offended if they say no.

I had a way of changing the subject that worked well for me when people would ask me how I was doing with my husband's cancer. If James or I was feeling overwhelmed or irritated with the direction of the conversation, I would often reply, "Denial is my happy place." Usually, this would create some laughter and lighten the room. Although this may sound like an odd response, the reality is that denying the realness and gravity of a difficult time is easy to do when you are in crisis or fight mode. Sometimes, telling your story can sidetrack a process of introspection that needs to take place for them. Not telling your experiences can be more beneficial in many ways so that when the patient has to put their voice to the telling of their present difficulty, many times, it can help them face their situation.

Denial is not faith. Faith is not denial. There is a vast difference.

On the other hand, stories of success or survival and overcoming illness such as cancer can be helpful if they are told without a hidden message because it is often what is implied that the hurting picks up. Timing is everything during a time like this. During the early stages of James's illness, we were all into listening to every person's experience; it was much less so at the end. Once again, timing is everything. One of the most challenging things I needed to do was call one of my "contact" friends in the last days of his life. As he hovered between this world and the next in a coma, we had come to an end. I needed to ask her to "please tell the people to stop praying for healing. Let him go. We cannot do this anymore. It is just too hard."

Do This Instead: More Acceptable Options

Any hope you can give is welcome, and any way that you are willing to crawl into the pit with us to help us out, we will embrace. But keep it real, keep it honest, and do not make the story you tell a parallel or a segue into a recitation of your own pain. To be frank, the most impactful testimonies were those that had been experienced firsthand and told with raw emotional impact and real fears that were felt during the process. Stories of events witnessed at miracle crusades or read from impactful books involving strangers were not quite as helpful. We wanted personal interaction with people whom we knew went through real problems and whom we could ask questions.

Telling the positive, hopeful events of your brother, wife, or child and building us up by reciting every time God intervened on your behalf is priceless! That is more helpful than you may ever know. We want to hear those stories! We actually need to listen to them in the beginning, in the middle, and in the end; but please be careful to watch our emotional cues. Although we may need to hear them, there may be times we are unable to do so.

Keep in mind that every situation is unique. Every illness, every crisis, and every trial is as dramatically different as the people who go through them. You may know those who have beaten the odds and come back from the brink of death. I believe that was God's plan for them, and I praise Him for it. Hallelujah! The individuals you know who have had those great healing stories do not know how this will end for us, and honestly, neither do you. If you believe God can heal, then I am led to believe that you are a praying person, so pray. Do it right then with them at the moment. Do not let the moment escape you! Pray on the phone or in person. Let them know that you are hoping for the best outcome but will stand with them in all the decisions they make, as well as in the ups and downs because there will be many.

The most important thing you can do is listen with your heart, and please *don't listen to respond*. Let the silence be weighty at times and make you a little uncomfortable. It is OK. Don't feel like you need to lighten the mood with a joke or some other kind of diversion that dismisses the uncomfortable reality. Instead, just listen to hear the heart of your friend, brother, sister, mother, or coworker. I realize it seems so ridiculous to say you are sorry because you have done nothing to cause the event before you. Yet it can be so very comforting to hear these words. Do not minimize your lack of words. Nobody is asking you to fix it.

A Few Words to the Caregiver and Patient

When many stories are thrown at you during the time you are in treatment or have hit the road of impasse, and it's beginning to sound like your doctors are losing hope for your case, please remember that these people are as uncomfortable about your illness, suffering, and diagnosis as you are, maybe even more so. My husband, James, was relatively young, which made our peers very uncomfortable. If it could happen to him, well … and who wants to think of that?

They are bringing their stories to give you hope, and they want you to get better! Your situation can make them feel very vulnerable about their own lives, health, or conditions. If you can gently move the conversation away from a testimony that makes you angry or uncomfortable, then do so. If you can't divert it, completely change the subject or speak kindly to what they are saying. You could say something like "I am sorry, I am unable to receive what you are saying at the moment. Maybe we could pick up this conversation on a different day." Or you could mention, "I need to think about what you are saying, and I think I may need to pray about some of it, but at the moment, I am struggling with some of what you are saying."

Be honest and straightforward in your kindness and leave the conversation there. Please change the subject and try not to engage in a discourse of defending your stand, opinion, or inability to hear them out. I got better at this as time went on. I realize how difficult it is to stop the flow of words when the storyteller is speaking, especially when they are trying to encourage you. However, if it doesn't sit well, it doesn't sit well. Continuing to listen will not make it feel any better. The key is not getting upset or arguing. Remembering that there are as many testimonies as there are people helped me to navigate my way through many of these uncomfortable tales. None of us can argue with someone else's experience, but if it isn't relatable to our own, we don't need to receive it either.

For my husband, who was such a gentle man, speaking up was something he learned to do for his own mental and physical health during his sickness. He was always so full of grace and mercy, and from that place, he would gently explain that he was tired and needed to rest or talk about something else that didn't take so much out of him. If he can learn this skill, so can you. It may not be easy, but it will be worth it.

Remember

For the caregiver/patient,

- Hold on to positive things you hear or learn by placing sticky notes around your home.
- Find a support group.
- Understand your facts and statistics to build you up and grow your faith.
- Have a notebook or journal.
- Write down questions you or others have and ask the doctor or nurses when you can.
- Write down answers and essential information so you can look back on it and relay it to others.
- Consider bringing a family member or close friend with you to doctor visits.
- Be kind but be honest.

Remember

Family, Friends, and Acquaintances

- Be sensitive with the questions you ask, and don't ask too many at one time.
- Be patient while you wait for answers, but also be gracious if the answers never come.
- Pay attention to the emotional state of the immediately affected, and move the conversation onto something less heavy.
- Offer to relieve them of some responsibilities. (Include a time when you are available.)
- Don't bring up that death will be a celebration or no more pain.
- Visit.
- Do not assume anything.
- Do not tell your horror stories.

CHAPTER 3

Common Questions

We tend to be a curious bunch of people. Whether the news is good or bad, we want details. Don't be surprised when you find yourself in the middle of your less-than-pleasant season, surrounded by many people with many questions. Finding yourself here can leave you answering the same thing multiple times to different people. You may find it true that many of these questions can grate on your nerves after a while, especially when you find yourself repeating yourself so much. However, there is also a positive side: they can actually help you sort through some deeper issues if you allow them to.

Just recently, I learned of a friend who was terminated from his job. Although he had been with the company for over thirty years, he was let go for a minor indiscretion. He should have been given the courtesy of an in-person meeting with the company's upper management. Instead, he received a phone call at his home in the evening, informing him that he could come in and retrieve his things from his office on the specified date. Utter devastation is what he felt, and various emotions choked his words when he called for prayer. I had a lot of questions and seemed as stunned as he did.

Confusion, frustration, and anxiety surfaced simultaneously as we talked. I felt for him in many ways, and although I had been terminated once many years ago, there was no comparison. I was all of twenty-five years old, and the job I lost was not my career. I knew I could only relate in the most minimal of ways, so I allowed him to lead the conversation. He spoke in detail as he tried to think of some reason why this had happened, all the while reeling from the loss of a pension, friends, and career. After letting him talk, I began to ask some gentle questions, such as "Do you think they will answer some of your questions if you called? What are you doing right now? Are you alone? Are you OK to be alone? What is your immediate next step?"

As he looked back, there were no valid reasons for dismissal; and as I have already stated, none were given. The people closest to him wanted to know why, which added to his frustration as time passed. What bothered him the most was the underlying, unvoiced suspicion of individuals as they found out what had happened. The often-unspoken yet hinted-at statement was that his employers must have been looking to get rid of him for a while, but why? This pervasive attitude cast suspicion on his character, morals, and work ethic. He was not perfect, and he knew that, but he was diligent and hardworking. He did his job with integrity and was well respected in his field.

It can be very common for us to look at the above scenario and think the man must have done something immoral, illegal, or vicious to receive this kind of treatment after all the years of service he had put in. Let's try to remember that our reactions affect those around us just as much as the things we say. I suddenly found myself thrust into this friend's pain when I brought him and his family up for prayer. When I explained the situation, I was met with a rather abrupt statement that held an undercurrent of not-so-hidden judgment. "There must be more to the story, so I'm going to pray about that!" He must have done something beyond what I had been told and that the Lord would reveal to my prying—I mean, praying—friend precisely what that was so she could "pray" more effectively for the one who lost the job.

I was shocked and slightly angered by the words that dimmed the integrity of the man in question until I began to ponder it. After some time of pondering and praying, I concluded that the questions we have come from a need to bring closure to challenging life events and that most of us do best when the things we are going through make sense. There are times, however, when things simply do not make sense. Unfortunately, life events often don't fit into those neat, labeled files we keep hidden in our minds; and therefore, we struggle.

I am sure there are reasons why this man was let go; one logical answer may be that after all those years, he was costing the company more in wages than they were willing to continue to pay. Of course, there may be other things that were at play, but knowing that, to date, he still has no satisfying answers from his former employer should help us settle the matter. Sometimes, we don't get answers to some of the most challenging things.

Remember the man I mentioned earlier whose wife underwent minor surgery that ended her life abruptly because of a doctor's error? That family wanted answers so they could have closure, and the reason they got was not one they wanted to hear. The event left devastation in all who were connected, myself included. As much as we dislike the thought, there will be times when there is no reason for why some things happen.

What is the reason? Why? Why is it that some people cannot conceive while others who can, abuse their children in horrific ways? Why is it that some children are born blind or with congenital disabilities? Why does one teen die in a car accident while the others walk away without a scratch? Why does a young family man end up with a devastating cancer that takes his life? Why do bad things happen to good people?

Sometimes, there are no answers, and we must learn to accept that fact so that we can love the hurting without adding more to the wound they already have. It may be best to leave our prying questions, along with our opinions and unspoken judgments, out of the conversation in the beginning so that the hurting will feel free to open up and find a place of healing. We should want them to feel safe enough to come and share, not make them want to run and hide.

In the leukemic world we were thrust into, we found we had many questions. This is where we quickly learned that not all our questions had answers. One of the problems was that we were without responses to other people's inquiries. The unfortunate part of this was that the questions we wanted answers to the most also seemed to be the ones without answers. One of those was that we wanted to know what made James susceptible to acute myeloid leukemia. The answer never did come, so we didn't get the closure we were looking for and still don't.

"I don't know. The doctors don't have any answers at this time," I heard myself respond to one of the several questions I had been asked so many times before. "How did he get leukemia?" "What treatments is he taking?" "Is he going for surgery?" "Will they do radiation and chemotherapy?" "How much longer will he be in the hospital?" "How are you doing?" "How are the kids doing?" "How are his parents handling this?" "What is his doctor's name?" "What kind of chemotherapy is he taking?" "Why does he need to go for bloodwork continually?" "Is he scared?" "Do you think he will die?"

These were some of the questions I was asked repeatedly throughout the fifteen months of his illness, often by the same people. The most pressing question was whether he was scared. It was a simple question to answer, and yet not simple at all. He was not afraid, and yet he was. I think most people have some level of timidity and trepidation when it comes to hearing the C word tagged onto their names. Whether you know God or not, the prospect of being that ill, with the possibility of death, is not exactly one you embrace with open arms and celebrate. Even as a believer in Christ, the idea of death carries weight. Death is final, and there is no do-over. Was he scared? Yes, there were times he was afraid, and there were times I was too.

Sometimes, I felt that it would be less daunting if I could prerecord the answers and press play when needed. There was nothing wrong with the questions, and I knew those who asked them cared about us and wanted to know what was happening, but it quickly became exhausting. Can I give you an example of what I mean? Have you ever ridden a roller coaster? If you have, you know what it is like to feel the pressure in your body as you are forced up a steep incline on the track or speed over the top of the crest to descend into the next turn or valley, feeling the weightlessness lift you off your seat. The twists and turns, the ups and downs, and the loops and spirals can leave you spinning. That is how it was, or at least how it sometimes felt. I desperately wanted to get off this unhappy ride but couldn't find the proverbial off switch so that I could disembark!

I had to learn some coping strategies to make it through, and one of the things I adopted was to leave texts unanswered until I was in a good-enough mental and emotional space to reply. Sorry to those of you who still have questions in cyberspace, but I did the best I could. I hope you can forgive me. Like you, James and I wanted answers; but more than that, we wanted solutions, which is another thing that we only sometimes get, regardless of how badly we may want them.

The truth is, no one seems to know "how" people "get" leukemia. Of course, there is some speculation and potential roots for the disease; but nothing, we were told, was concrete evidence. It is unlike other cancers in many ways, and my husband ended up being a case study because of the aggressiveness of his disease.

Leukemia is a broad term for a type of blood cancer that can be very slow-acting or very aggressive. It can affect anyone at any age. Your chances of getting it are not lessened by being active and healthy, a vegan, or a positive person. At least, that is what we were told. Leukemia is not selective with its victims; the nurses would often say it was the "nice person's cancer" because it seemed like those who got it were the nicest people they met. I have no idea whether this is a reality, but they all insisted it was, and James was a very nice person.

There is a more pressing issue here that I would like to bring up regarding asking questions. Some people need information because they are genuinely invested in the person who is ill or going through something. Then, there are those who are not. It seemed like some people asking questions were looking for ways to receive information so they could keep up-to-date with what was happening without getting emotionally or physically engaged. It was as if they had no more interest or investment than that of knowing more for themselves or engaging others in discussion. In short, they didn't want to help or support in any way; they only wanted to know what was happening and how everyone was doing. This is not necessarily wrong, especially if you desire to pray; but if you want to be up-to-date with what is happening, perhaps you can find a way to receive information secondhand rather than from those directly in it. Being sensitive to this is vital because the caregiver, family, or person suffering often gets tired of repeatedly answering the same questions.

In order to explain the levels of information needed or wanted, I will give a scenario that will help you understand how those most directly involved might feel when you come armed with inquiries.

Have you ever had something happen to you that required you to recite your story of the events to multiple people? I will use the parallel of a car accident to help get my point across. When you have been in a car wreck, you must answer the same questions multiple times to multiple people. The police officer who will undoubtedly be involved is someone of authority who will question you to help them determine probable causes. He or she will want to know what happened, where you were, what you were doing, if you were distracted or turning, and how fast you were going. Everything they will ask you is necessary, but they only have one purpose. The police officer wants to know precisely what happened to determine who is in the wrong, if charges need to be pressed, and who should be charged. The officer asks many questions but is not invested in you.

They will help you get the emergency care you need, but they are not and will not be supportive in your long-term recovery if you should need it. This interaction is not personal. It is a required interrogation for specific legal purposes.

On the other hand, if this scenario played out in your life—and hopefully, it doesn't—your parent or spouse would likely ask the same questions. Except it would feel very different. You would be aware of their genuine concern for your overall welfare. They would hopefully be much less worried about the state of the vehicle, who was in the wrong, or how it happened. The exact same questions will likely be asked, but the love and care you feel will provoke a different response within you as you feel the empathy, love, and concern, as well as their desire and willingness to help you in any way possible. This is the same difference that those going through a tough time feel when the same questions are presented to them from various sources. They may sound the same, but they feel different because they are different.

At no time should the questions you ask the struggling person make them feel like you are doing nothing more than gathering data. It should never feel to them like you are trying to determine the cause of the illness, divorce, job loss, or other difficulty they are enduring. Nor should they be made to feel like they are solely responsible for their demise, and their emotions should never be overlooked or dismissed. Emotions are a huge part of everything we go through, both good and bad; but in challenging situations, they cannot be ignored, just as there are times when emotions cannot be stifled for a few hours until there is the time to release the tears.

Unfortunately, we do not know how to support well those who are struggling emotionally, physically, or spiritually because we have not been taught to do so. How do you encourage the brokenhearted without silencing them? How do we take the load off the shoulders of someone who needs it without telling them to get over themselves because that shuts them down? How do we listen? How long do we listen before we lose patience and tell them to stop the pity party, look for the silver lining in their hurricane, and think happy thoughts?

Our questions, responses, and presentations all tell them a story, especially when they are in pain. In our quest for answers, which we feel will help satisfy our *why*, we can come across more like the police officer in this chapter than a loving friend. I acknowledge that this can be a very fine line, but honest concern and compassion can be felt, and love is always welcome. So fill your questions with these components, and you should be just fine.

Society

I have lived my entire life in Canada and am so blessed to have been able to do so. The country is alive with wildlife, prairies, mountains, and four distinct seasons, with temperature fluctuations to prove the point. The trees are brilliant in fall, the sunsets are alive on the prairies, and the oceans are magnificent! It is a blessed country of freedom, equality, adventure, promise, and opportunity.

With all the positives, you would think we had it made; but Canada, like other free countries, has some me-centric issues that cannot be ignored. It often seems like much of the focus is on having a good time because we have been taught that we should be as happy and fulfilled as possible. I mean, why not? You deserve it! It is everywhere we look. Media portrays this in many commercials we watch, from beer around the campfire, tropical holidays we are told we deserve, dinner on the town, and bubble baths with a glass of wine in hand after a hard day at the office. We deserve luxury, we have earned a break, and we deserve happiness. All we need to do is look at others around us and see the houses, cars, and vacations they enjoy. Whether we want to admit it or not, commercials like these do shape our thinking.

This subtle standard for how our lives should be lived also bleeds into the movies we watch. Most often, the plots in our favorite movies are so similar you can tell the end from the beginning without a preview. There is a struggle, emotional or physical pain, and heart-wrenching decisions to be made. As the movie progresses and we crest the peak of the story, we end with the best-case scenario and a happy-ever-after ending, and we like it that way!

However realistic it may seem, this kind of life plot on screen is fiction; and it rarely, if ever, happens this way in the long-term. I am sorry to burst your bubble. Being inundated with this kind of entertainment has caused many of us to file things in our minds in the way we like them and how we want them to go, which can translate to "the way it *should* be." Except it isn't. Life sometimes has a different feel and often ends differently than in the feel-good Christmas specials because life is messy and complicated, and sometimes there are no good answers.

It is when we come face-to-face with illness, disease, job loss, death, bankruptcy, third-world poverty, child trafficking, and many other things that we realize there is much more beyond our feel-good moments. Although we have been heavily indoctrinated by the things we watch and listen to, we live in a real world with real-world problems. Sometimes, these real-world problems come knocking on our doors or that of our neighbors. When it does, we must try to think and feel outside of the box or of what we have been taught, and leave our me-centricity behind. This includes the thinking that all will end well if we will just look at things positively. What we should do or, may I suggest, must do is be compassionate and meet them where they are at. Sit with them there and be the ear and shoulder they need.

For those of us who come from a faith background, the tendency is to blame life's hardships on wrongdoing, past sins, karma, or some other law of attraction. These laws have a universal thinking to them, but essentially, they all say the same thing: you deserve what you are going through; but if you change, your circumstances will correct themselves, and then you will be fully restored. Other practices believe that whatever happens to you is because God knows you can handle it. Now that is a real "buck it up, buttercup" statement! If God knows you can do it, get up and get moving. There is no room for emotions.

I believe that all people are created in God's image; therefore, we will all be drawn to believe in something, even if it is an adamant belief that there is no God. However, I also think that if we allow what we believe about our faith background or the popular teachings of society to guide us instead of coming from a loving relationship with our God, we will appear cold and harsh. Approaching others armed with that kind of aloofness and intellectual place will likely ensure an abysmal reception to questions. Do you want to be as impersonal as the police officer or as caring as the family of those involved in the car accident? We don't want to portray to the person(s) in difficulty that there is little interest in how they are doing, but more on if they are "doing it right! (according to us, anyway)."

But what does "doing it right" look like? I think that depends on whom you ask, what they have gone through in their past life experiences, how they live their religion, or even if they have a religious system they lean on. My past experiences tell me that prayer works! I can wholeheartedly attest to that. I have seen God answer prayer in remarkable ways, even miraculous ways, and I have also seen what appears to be "unanswered prayers." I have seen sick people recover, and I have seen them die. I have witnessed monetary needs met, and I have seen them not met. The truth is, if you have been a believer for any length of time, you could say the same. But would you?

We must be honest and not only shine the light on the positivity of what we *want* to believe because it is what we have been taught to believe and rely upon, which is a replacement for the truth, which proves the opposite evidence as fact. We should not determine the end result of a current situation because of past miracles we have witnessed without admitting that it doesn't always work out that way. Faith is faith, and I have faith! Glorification of a God, universe, or karma who only does what we want is not faith in God. That is faith in what we want to believe.

We must be willing to accept that what we believe is absolute or admit it is not. If I believe that God is who He says He is and He is purposeful in the things He does, then I must also believe that that includes those things that I do not understand, even when it hurts. The truth is that there are things we will want to know and questions we will not get answers to this side of eternity. For those of you who believe in Jehovah, the God in the Holy Bible, all we need to do is take a little stroll through Hebrews 11 and the book of Revelation, for example. We will quickly see that there is not always a best-case scenario.

I don't mean to be a Debbie Downer, but having faith in God and who He is means that we believe in the promises He has given, whether we see them manifested or not. It means we accept He is who He says He is and, therefore, will do what only He can do! If we can trust that He is good and His promises are for us and our good, then we can accept the good and the not so good.

Positive Thinking

I feel like I am treading on some sacred cows in this chapter, but I will push ahead anyway because I believe we can do a much better job of supporting one another than we have in the past. I am generally a decently positive person, but I would also describe myself as a realist. I believe in speaking positively in the sense that I am not criticizing, condemning, judging, and constantly finding faults. I do believe we should be looking for the gold in others, not the dirt. I also believe we should stay as positive as possible as we roll through the waves of sickness, disease, and loss.

There are times I don't believe that positive speaking or positive thinking is the answer to the problem in difficult life situations. I give this topic its own space because it needs to be individually addressed. Positive speaking was an all-too-common theme throughout the fifteen months of my husband's illness, and very often, any one of us in the family felt the chastening that this kind of thinking could bring. We need to be careful with our mouths because out of them proceed the things hidden and embedded in our hearts. "For the mouth speaks out of that which fills the heart" (Matthew 12:34 AMP).

Having said that, speaking positively without faith in God to accomplish a thing is just positive talk. However, I also want to note that I don't believe that positive speaking indicates faith because I have seen many times where it has produced a "work harder" mentality. Many people wanted us to never speak of his illness, the doctors' reports of doom, or the possibility of death because James would live if we only spoke positively. This is magical thinking. If the results I seek have more to do with everything I need to do, then is it faith? If I believe harder, pray more, confess those things more, et cetera, then I will receive what I believe in. It doesn't sound like restful faith, does it? Hebrews 4 tells us we are to do all things from a place of rest, not work. "There remains therefore a rest for the people of God. For he who has entered His rest has himself also ceased from his works as God did from His. Let us therefore be diligent to enter that rest, lest anyone fall according to the same example of disobedience" (Hebrews 4:9–11). Working harder will not necessarily guarantee you a miracle. We should trust Him and believe that when we pray, He hears us; and if He hears us, He will answer—trust, rest, and faith.

"This is the [remarkable degree of] confidence which we [as believers are entitled to] have before Him: that if we ask anything according to His will, [that is, consistent with His plan and purpose] He hears us. And if we know [for a fact, as indeed we do] that He hears and listens to us in whatever we ask, we [also] know [with settled and absolute knowledge] that we have [granted to us] the requests which we have asked from Him" (1 John 5:14,15).

Then, accept your result.

To clear up any misconceptions, positive thinking and positive speaking are vital to your overall well-being as long as it is not toxic positivity. Toxic positivity is more like denial, and that isn't helpful at all. I have seen it cross boundaries to such extremes that there is no room for any comment that is not hyperpositive, leaving little room for reality. We all have down days from time to time; but when your world falls apart, own it, accept it, and do not stuff it under the guise of overly joyous words that conceal the pain deep inside you. Did you know that if you don't deal with your negative emotions, it can directly affect your health? Please don't fall into this kind of positivity.

I believe that positive thinking and speaking can also be rooted in faith, and when it is, the spoken words can carry an element of power that changes things. I have seen this happen many times. God speaks to His children, and when you have that as your foundation, don't back down. You can never be more positive than God, so don't try to work it up and make it happen. Just rest in what He has said as you speak. Positive speaking is a popular teaching in many areas of society, not just in the church, so it can be a problematic bullet to dodge. We faced it regularly from various people, and it sometimes became a thorn in the flesh. Being told we were not to speak the doctors' reports or relay what was said from the stem cell transplant team, or that his body was beginning to fail because that was negative, was nothing short of ridiculous. I would look at the man I had known for over thirty years sitting on our loveseat—yellow, pale, and sweating—knowing he was unable to eat and was nauseous and feeling pain. If I had followed this advice, I couldn't talk about it because it was negative, and that wouldn't have helped any of us, especially him.

The truth is, we were optimistic, had faith, and believed that God could move in the circumstances we faced and heal James. We trusted his life was in God's hands whether he lived or died, and we prayed fervently that it would be the first of the two. We were told that you cannot have faith and be afraid. I am not sure if that is true, although it certainly seems easy to say, especially for those without experience. I believe we had both. We had faith, but there were times when we were afraid. We were emotionally normal throughout the journey, and I suspect you will be too! Perhaps we can be scared, trust God, and do it or go through it anyway?

If you are a believer and follower of Jesus Christ, may I suggest that before you come in telling others how they should be handling their crisis, you begin by asking questions of Him in prayer. "What do you want from me in this situation, and how can I benefit my friend most at this time?" There may be times when they need the pep talk to bring them out of despair and hopelessness that helps them pull up their bootstraps and begin to fight once more, but there are also times when they may just need someone to lean on. You can be the person they need in either situation, and as you let them lean on you, they might begin to allow you to shoulder the burden with them and enable you to help them with some of the things around the home that are currently being overlooked. This might seem like an insignificant gesture, but it carries much weight.

When my husband began to deteriorate (from the end of July through to his passing on September 9), we were spending the full eight to twelve hours a day in the outpatient ward at least five days a week. When his spleen suddenly became enlarged, he spent one week in the hospital, which gave us a break from traveling because the regular blood work panel and infusions of platelets, potassium, antibiotics, and magnesium that could keep us at the U of A Hospital all day would be done while he was admitted.

As a side note, we were all exhausted before his admittance for the final nine days, but during that time and without my knowledge, one of my neighbors faithfully cut my lawn. To this day, I have no idea who it was, and they all deny it, but I know someone did it. That simple gesture was thoughtful, practical, and very, very appreciated. Thank you so much to whoever you are!

Common Questions

Some of the questions that were asked bear repeating. Although you realize I have already put these on paper once, this is the unfortunate reality of people going through the wringer: "How did he get leukemia?" "What are the treatments?" "Is he going for surgery?" "How much longer will he be in the hospital this time?" "How are you doing?" "How are the kids doing?" "What about his parents?" "What is his doctor's name?" "What kind of chemotherapy is he taking?" "Why does he need to go for blood work continually?" "Is he afraid?" "Do you think he will die?"

Do you think he will die?—that was a good question, but do you know the old saying, "If I had a dollar for every time"? You know what I am saying if you have ever been or are in a similar situation, because I think if I had made a dollar for every time this question was asked, I would have made a little hard, cold cash. Although it was a good question, and one I understood why others were asking, it wasn't so easily answered. We found that in the beginning, the doctors were not committed to answering it; but as time passed and the evidence became more evident, they would adamantly stand on the prognosis that death would be the end result. This statement was so incredibly difficult to hear when it was finally said! Understand that this is gut-wrenchingly impossible to wrap your head, heart, or emotions around. It never got easier to hear, either.

I didn't want this question asked. I didn't want to speak the words because I didn't want to admit it. Yet this was a continual inquiry, and very often, it brought with it emotional tidal waves that rolled in, crashing and destroying any peace I had left within me! I wasn't trying to be difficult by not looking at the facts as they were presented. But considering the chaos that was swirling around us regarding his health and the expectations of those around us on how to "properly" navigate this unknown ground, I was unsure what to say.

With everything inside of me, I wanted to say no, he wasn't going to die, but I wasn't so sure that I believed he would live; after all, I had had that dream. The honest answer was yes. Yes, I think he will die. Yes, he will die. But that answer is brutal! That answer is hard, cold, and final. It steals hope, and to be completely fair, that is a question no one wants to answer honestly. I kept to the same answer for most people, except for a select few whom I felt I could be vulnerable with and still be accepted. My standard response was "I don't know. I am praying with you that he doesn't."

Keeping this in mind, please be gracious if your questions remain unanswered. I don't mean to be harsh with this following statement, but I don't know how else to frame it, but what you ask may be less important than how you ask it. If you lack experience in hardships, your speech will betray you, and your preconceived ideas on how to handle problems will be seen for what they are. People going through hard times tend to be able to read the hearts of people around them, so be honest and genuine. Be vulnerable enough to tell them you don't know how to respond or act. Let them know you are afraid of putting your foot in your mouth and saying the wrong things, but don't try to find or give answers to questions that may not have answers.

It is also important to remember that the most prominent and most challenging questions were not asked of you. The hard questions were asked of your hurting loved ones. They have the monumental task of wading through it all and coming to terms with the information presented to them. They have the most to lose, the most emotional turmoil to process, and the most questions to answer; so they may not be able to do so at the time with you. Questions regarding care, treatments, next steps, and living wills were not asked of you; therefore, the responses are not yours to give. Instead of giving advice, please sincerely provide your support, love, and empathy because these things are always welcome and received.

A Few Words to the Caregiver and Patient

If you haven't already found this to be true, you will quickly find out that these and many other questions will be common to you and your circle of friends. Some will be unique to you, your situation, your group, and your culture, while others are more universally asked. As someone who has heard many, I certainly have not heard all, nor do I want to; there are some expected questions consisting of "How are you doing?" "How are they doing?" or "How are the kids, parents?" You may find that these questions will come at you from almost every conversation you have, including your doctors. Preparing yourself with an answer for any situation is helpful, even when it gets on your last nerve, which it likely will.

Acknowledging that not everyone needs a full, in-depth answer will help, so let's take some time to help you categorize how much information to share and who needs to "know that information." Separating those who genuinely want to know from those who ask as if it was part of an everyday conversation may help. Not everyone deserves the same information from you, especially if it will take away emotional support from others who need it. "Hi, it is so good to see you. How are you?" We all do it. Until your moment of crisis, this question was just a polite way to begin a conversation that helps them get caught up on life events, but once you enter the realm of uncertainty and upheaval in your life, it feels different. It seems to hold more weight. How do you answer this? You may even find yourself slipping out the usual past responses you have always given, such as "I am great!" "Fine" or "Couldn't be better!" However, it just won't work anymore, and when you say it, you feel the impact of your words in a way that you are unaccustomed to.

How do you navigate this one? At one point, my husband was so tired of the question, overwhelmed with his situation, and on a day when he wasn't feeling well that he blurted out, "I'm dying. How do you think I'm doing?" His quick, honest, but harsh retort hit the room like a bomb went off, silencing everyone in it and making it incredibly awkward for a while! I find it humorous on this side of his comment, but even I was taken aback by his statement at the time! To clarify, this is not the most effective way of handling it, even if I understand where it comes from.

You may find that there is a lot of pressure placed on you as you go through rough times in life, but if you can look at it as a period of intense growth, it might help. Don't get me wrong. I am in no way suggesting that you are going through what you are going through because you need to learn something. When you get the news of illness, divorce, job loss, or some other massive change, try to prepare yourself to be hit by many things you have not yet experienced. Some of the things you will be faced with might include paperwork, legal papers, courts, hospitals, information overload, emotional upheaval, stress, fears, and decisions that need to be made that you don't want to make. You may, and probably will, be pushed too quickly through some of these decision-making processes, which may make you feel overwhelmed and out of control.

Understanding that you will be asked "How are you doing?" far more often than you would like should help you mentally and emotionally prepare to answer acceptably. Take the time to think about it. Ask yourself that question, "How will I answer the next time it is asked of me?" Having what I like to call a "push play" answer can certainly help alleviate some of the awkwardness in trying not to divulge more than you deem necessary. You may be asking, "What is a push-play answer?" It is the standard answer you repeat without having to think in the moment. This answer should help cover all the information you want to divulge without causing you to lose your composure or go more in-depth than you want to.

I observed from our situation that four basic types of people would ask this question. You may decide to give varying levels of the truth to each group, and no, I am not talking about being deceptive but instead protecting yourself and your loved ones. By taking this approach, you control how the conversation goes, which is entirely acceptable because not everyone is in your inner circle. They do not need to know the in-depth details. Responding like this allows you to base your responses on your ability to cope with what you can handle at the time because not everyone needs to know everything. When you realize that your answers usually lead to more questions, you can decide how many questions you want to open yourself up to during the initial conversations. Thinking about this beforehand can release you from human expectations. Remember, you have to reserve your emotional and physical strength for other more pressing conversations that you must have. Sometimes, your responses to each person as to how it will benefit and protect, not emotionally harm, you and your loved ones must be evaluated.

I will briefly break down the four levels of communication you will face and, hopefully, give you some valuable tips on dealing with each one.

1. Those Who Don't Really Want Details but Are Being Polite in Conversation

You will quickly find that this is the most extensive group of individuals that you will come across. It includes, but is not limited to, acquaintances and work friends. The number of people in your circle of influence will determine the number of people who will want to connect, and this number can vary greatly. However, I found that this is one of the most manageable groups to navigate and the easiest to use, the "push play" response, thus guiding the conversation in the safest way for your needs.

The individuals in this group are made up of people who may be genuinely interested in how you are doing, but they only need to know some of the details. Giving them the basics is best. Answering the questions about how you are feeling overall and how you are dealing with the stress can be handled efficiently with your scripted response. In short, they want you to know that you are being thought of, are concerned for you, and care about what happens to you. As you quickly respond by filling in the basics and highlighting one or two points, you should be able to move on in the conversation. When faced with anyone from within this group, I found it easiest to be polite, which kept me unemotional. Letting them know they could spread the news I shared with them to their field of influence also shortened my ever-growing to-do list.

Many conversations within this group left us feeling uplifted, encouraged, and not criticized. For some reason that I cannot explain, most, but not all, of these individuals were very respectful of our time. Often, the visitation was a diversion to the ugly things we were facing and enabled us to laugh and chitchat about what was going on in the workplace as we engaged in a little friendly workplace gossip. Laughter was often found in abundance, while the short visits were very doable for James, who tended to tire quickly as the months passed.

2. Those Who Need Details but Don't Need to Know How You Are Emotionally (Employers, Supervisors, and Human Resources)

Conversations within this circle can be much more detail-oriented and factual while you remain emotionally detached, if possible. The information you present when asked "How are you doing?" or "What is happening?" should provide any new details that they must have access to. During the initial hospital admission for James and for quite some time afterward, he was well able to speak with his employer, supervisors, and human resources directly, keeping them up-to-date with his progress. I was then free to keep in contact with mine, but as his health fluctuated wildly, I was forced to have an in-depth conversation with my employer that led to me being on caregiver leave just four months into his illness.

I suggest this if it is doable. This category of individuals needs more than rudimentary information; they need to understand what is happening and how the doctors predict it will play out. They may need access to doctors' reports if they need to file for disability, so they can help you file for caregiver's aid or other aids you may qualify for. This could mean they may have more questions than you have thought of or might be prepared emotionally or intellectually to answer. When you need to supply the information you don't have, remember to have your trusted notepad and pen handy to jot it down so you can send it to them when you can.

James and I were incredibly thankful that our employers, HR, and supervisors worked with us. Although the companies we worked for were quite large, the groups of people we worked with daily were small, and we were in constant contact with those in management before his illness. With the friendships that were built because of previous close contact, we were handled with gentleness and concern, which, I acknowledge, isn't always the case.

3. Those Who Need Details and Facts (Immediate Family and Close Friends)

Individuals in this group will undoubtedly be the most emotionally charged of all the people you will have to deal with. Talking with them as you discuss the details won't always be easy because of their investment and love for you and your loved one. Families and very close friends are the most affected by your situation and are invested in your life and what you are going through. They want the truth, but they also deserve the truth! What you may find, as I did, is that they have many more questions than anyone else; and they want answers to all of them, which you may only sometimes be able to provide. Knowing this can be helpful, but it may also be frustrating.

Group number three may have questions you have yet to think of asking, so jotting them down will help in the long run. However, each question you answer will stir up further questions within them or perhaps within yourself. For me, the stream of questions they had often seemed unending, and I was never fully prepared for all of them, especially the ones posed by his immediate family. The critical thing to remember is that this group loves you, your family, and everyone involved. It is because of this that it can feel like they want too much information or be too involved, but they are not.

Being the kind of person I am, I wanted to try to shield both his parents and especially our children from the harshness of the truth, especially when James and I were not doing very well emotionally or physically. We needed to learn how to speak the truth in a way that was easier to hear, such as "You know, it's hard. Sometimes, I'm [he's] OK, and sometimes I am [he's] not OK. Today I [he] is …" Although it can be easy to get very self-focused during this time, it was also imperative that we did a wellness check on them as well because this is an arduous journey for those most closely involved.

I can't tell you when it happened, but there was a time when I released myself from the expectations to know everything that was happening. On the other hand, my personality is one that needs to know. Once a question was asked, I was willing to find the answer, if possible. I found my tenacity in this area to be to our benefit more than a few times. Because of the closeness of the relationships, James and I were willing to look at options to help us help them find their answers. So when James was in the hospital, I could invite his parents or sister to be in the room when the doctors made their rounds. It was a tactic that ended up being wonderful; although they couldn't always visit because of work restrictions and travel time, it gave them the opportunity to ask their questions and get answers directly from the doctors. James also permitted the oncologists to speak directly with his parents to help them better understand exactly what was going on.

You will find your way, and you will find what works best for you and your family. Having said that, for many people, family can be the most frustrating to deal with. But you will learn the best way to handle everyone involved, even if it means using a third person to assist you in communicating the news.

4. Your Doctors, Nurses, and Home Care

You may be wondering why I am including this group of individuals because you would think this goes without saying, but honestly, it does need to be addressed. When anyone in this group asks you how you or they (the person who is ill) are doing, they ask because they can help you! The absolute truth must always be told here, so get gritty and brutally honest in explaining what is happening. They need to know! If you are not doing well emotionally, they need to know. If you are not doing well psychologically, they need to know. If you are deteriorating in any way with your health or if there are changes of any kind, they need to know!

Putting on a stiff upper lip may seem heroic, but they can't support you if you are not honest. There may be times when you don't like what is going on. For example, you may not want to be hospitalized again, take more treatment, or go for more tests. The reality of the length of time this can take may be frustrating, as can your loss of physical strength. You may be afraid of being very ill with side effects to the drugs you must take, or you may be afraid to die. This is normal! Most people struggle with these things at some juncture in their lives. But knowing that they understand your situation better than you do because this is not their first merry-go-round should help you be honest. Your honesty will enable them to point you in the right direction for the kind of help you may need.

This was a relatively common scenario in Ward 5 of the U of A Hospital, and it was definitely something James and I argued about more often than I thought necessary. He was always Mr. Positive and never wanted to be the center of attention, so he would often downplay his illness. I hadn't realized how much he was doing this until his sister asked me why she seemed to get a very different report when she talked to James than when she spoke to me. As I explored the question with him, I discovered he didn't want to upset anyone, so he told her and his parents what they wanted to hear: he was doing fine, great even, and no, the doctors hadn't said anything new. When I discovered this was what he had been doing, I would do my best to be at the hospital for rounds while he was an inpatient. I also decided it would be best for me to be at every oncologist appointment from that point forward. He was upset about this, but we all needed and wanted to know exactly what was being said regarding his health and care.

I can honestly say that there were a few heated moments when I had to interrupt his conversation with the doctors to explain that he was, in fact, "not fine!" There were times when my "tattling" on him would lead to him being admitted to the hospital, which would anger him. On the other hand, I would be relieved knowing that he was in the right place for the kind of care I could not give him at home.

As I end this chapter about questions, I want to ask those of you who are prone to pose questions to the hurting: why are you asking the question? You may find this bold and slightly uncomfortable, but it is a valid question. What is it you want to know, and how much information do you want? Once you have pinpointed your *why*, proceed with caution. Be specific but not intrusive. Make sure to let them know that you don't need all the information and that you are OK if they don't want to answer. Either way, be prepared to end up with much more conversation, information, and perhaps very detailed and intimate information than you bargained for. You may also get much, much less than you want, so settle that in your heart before talking to those suffering. Let them know you will be OK with the information you receive, if any, understanding that they may be emotionally taxed that day. After they have divulged what they want or not, work on being OK with the information you receive.

We all have so much to learn when it comes to knowing how to support other people through the difficulties of life. We are always young enough to learn or understand new things that might help us become more supportive and caring. You will always do right by loving another person and meeting them where they are. Remember, some of the best things you can do is just be their friend, cook that meal, mow that lawn, buy a gas card, or take up a collection to help with expenses. These are things that will more than likely never be asked of you but are so very, very appreciated.

Remember

- Try to keep your questions to a minimum.
- Let your concern and love lead your questions.
- Be compassionate.
- Be positive in the face of adversity, but don't have "magical thinking."
- Ditch toxic positivity.
- Allow yourself to do needed jobs without acknowledgment.
- Be OK if there are no answers to your questions.
- Be honest about what you believe about your situation.
- Be honest about your struggle with your belief system.
- Ask yourself why you are asking the question. What do you want to know, and why?

CHAPTER 4

The Comparison Trap

Have you ever done a self-evaluation? How about a job interview? Few things are more fear-inducing these days than sitting before a potential new employer and answering questions that make you uncomfortable. "Can you please just ask me if I am qualified for the job, if I have experience, and how well I work with a team?" During the interview process, we can become self-conscious or feel inadequate, which may be one of the things they are looking for. But there is also something else to consider: does the line of questioning during this time lead you to compare yourself to someone else? If it does, you don't stand alone. There can be a lot of anxiety over moments like these, and your inadequacies can surface during the interview.

Moments like these and many others we go through can normalize comparing ourselves with others. For example, in North America, the cloak of comparison seems to cover us from the moment of our conception. The comments come so quickly, easily, and joyfully as young moms-to-be discuss how the pregnancy is going. Questions tend to revolve around whether you have morning sickness and how long you have had it. Is your baby active in utero or very relaxed and peaceful, and do you have stretch marks or not? These are very normal conversations to be had during this time. It creates a bonding experience among expectant moms as they discuss common discomforts and remedies on how best to relieve heartburn and aching backs. First-time moms can be nervous, excited, and a little unsure, so conversations that lead to encouragement are lovely and much needed. And then, the babies come.

I am not the first to point out that comparing ourselves with others isn't helpful or healthy, and it will have one of two effects on us: we will either feel better or worse about ourselves on how we are doing than we did before. Judging ourselves against others only works if we feel better about ourselves when finished, but isn't that the reason we do it in the first place? We want to measure our abilities against someone else's disabilities, our talents against someone else's lack of talent, and so on. But the truth is this: comparison comes from insecurities about ourselves and how we do things, look, sound, act, parent, cook, clean, or a thousand other things. In the example I have just given about first-time moms, the comparison makes you feel better only if you are the woman who, for instance, hasn't gained an extra fifty pounds.

Parenting is hard enough without looking over your shoulder all the time, wondering if you or your child is being judged. Things like intelligence, talent, common sense, emotions, temper tantrums, obedience, rebellion, and eating are just a few of the ways we judge one another as we compare our children's abilities, as well as our parenting styles. I thank God that part of my life is over as I pat myself on the back for a job decently done. I couldn't be prouder of my children and their achievements. Comparison is not a pretty word.

I did a little research on this subject and found that, according to some studies, it is estimated that as much as 10 percent of our daily thinking involves comparisons! That may not sound like a lot at first glance, but it comes to a whopping two hours and twenty-four minutes per day! I have often justified this behavior, and you may have as well. One reason we compare ourselves with others might be the untruth that we are strengthening an area of our lives that may need improvement, but it can also have the opposite effect. It can steal your motivation, hope, or joy and make you feel worthless and incapable.

Another reason we may do it often comes from a desire to self-evaluate. Many of us have a need to understand things about ourselves to better embrace our purpose for being alive here on planet Earth. We may think that if we can know our strengths and weaknesses, we might be able to figure out which career path to take. It can also help us settle some of our personality quirks. Self-evaluation can help us heal a broken, abusive, or abandoned past; take the chance to love those around us; and even forgive those who have hurt us.

Validation is something we need throughout our lives, not just as children. However, many of us were not given much of this confidence-boosting applause when we were growing up and needed it most. That need will leave a perpetual hole in us. When something happens that rubs against that lack of validation and self-assurance, we will feel insecure. When we feel insecure or rejected, the need for validation will surface and lead us to look at those people most similar to us as a standard to help us determine what we are doing well and what areas need improvement. However, this sets up a playing field that is not level because our past and present experiences are usually vastly different. Let's not forget about our personalities and coping mechanisms, which are also contributing factors. For these reasons and more, when we compare ourselves to others, it usually doesn't work out in any helpful way.

Parenting is universal, and although some cultures have differences unique to their own countries and beliefs, the basic principles are the same. Kids do best when they have structure, discipline, and loads of love; this makes them feel safe and builds self-confidence. Although we know this and may even have some confidence in our parenting abilities, we still tend to observe how others do it so that we can validate our own practices. In particular, we look at what could be done better to see how those actions could be detrimental to the child later in life. There is a significant flaw in this strategy, however, and it is that it is easy to lose sight of the fact that there are factors we know nothing about. If you are a believer and follower of Christ, you should acknowledge that all people are created in the image of Almighty God, who has a plan for all of us. Knowing this means going beyond our parenting styles. If you believe this is true for you and your children, can you also trust that His purposes extend to those around you as well? I recognize that this may be a very simplistic way of looking at things—and indeed, it is among the most basic—but the truth remains.

If you believe that He is the author of your life, then you must accept that He will take care of the details, even if, and especially when, the road gets rough. If we honestly believe He has a plan for our lives and our families, then let's work on extending that same grace to those around us. I have watched parents who were negligent addicts raise children who serve and love the Lord, knowing full well that this should not have been how it turned out, but it did. The children's future did not wholly rest upon what the parents did correctly but instead upon the grace of God. This reveals that He is, indeed, more significant than our mistakes. I am not overlooking the truth that those same children who are serving the Lord do have some hurts from their past that need to be healed because of the abuses, but again, God is more than able to do it.

What I want to convey, and what I want us to understand, is that every one of us is unique in every way. I would like us to consider that how we live our lives and the belief systems we embrace reflect that uniqueness. With this in mind, it can be beneficial and very releasing when we understand that the person we are created to be is meant to reflect an image of God in the very things we go through, whether they be delightful or challenging. Let us be as willing and as prepared as possible to make the most of every opportunity, both pleasant and adverse, without comparing ourselves to how someone else is doing it or did it.

You may be asking yourself why I added parenting in a book called *What Not to Say*. Let me explain. I added what seems to be something unrelatable because we have all known comparisons of this kind. We have all felt the judgment and critical comments of others as children, and if you are a parent, you can recount your stories of the comparisons that came your way when it was your child in aisle five of the grocery store having a meltdown.

I was always the smallest kid in the class in height and weight, and I was teased relentlessly while my parents were often judged for it. Through the years, nothing much has changed; and except on a rare occasion, I am still the shortest among my group of friends. The difference is I am OK with who I am now. I also have a son who has ADHD, and through his many growing-up years, there were far too many comments that came both of our ways. He is now doing very well, but we did have quite a few struggles. For those of you going through this with your child, you understand what I am saying.

I included this scenario for another reason, and that is so you would remember how it feels to get caught up on the bottom end of the comparison and that it doesn't feel good when you feel like you are doing it wrong, especially when you are trying your hardest. Do you remember a time when you felt good about your accomplishments until someone came along with a negative comment or two and changed how you viewed what you had worked so hard to achieve? It is not helpful.

I wish the comparisons ended here, but unfortunately, it doesn't. While every person will deal with the difficulties they are handed during their lifetime in their own unique way, the comparisons will, unfortunately, follow them into these moments as well. Things like how they are handling the pressure they are under, the information they have been given in diagnosis, or any doctor's appointment that may have upset the balance. There will likely be a scrutinizer hidden in the nearby proverbial bushes. I wish this wasn't true. But I heard many people tell me that if they had cancer, they knew what they would do, they knew what kind of treatment they would take, and the faith stand they would make. What I do know, from our experience, is you do not! You won't know how you will react or what your next steps will be until your doctor pulls their chair up to touch yours, looks you in the eyes, tells you the truth, and presents you with a plan on how they wish to proceed. Only then will you know how to handle this situation.

When my husband became ill and spent sixty-six days in the hospital, we got to know a few people in the ward. These were people of all ages with varying degrees of severity regarding their specific blood disease. As we talked to many of them, we found that some had families while others did not. There were businesspeople, farmers, and homemakers; and they all had a story to tell about how they had lived their lives, why they made the choices they had made in the past, and how that seemed to shape their current situation. Every person was as different as the jobs they held and the ethnic backgrounds they came from, but they all had one thing in common. Every man, woman, and young adult in Ward 5 had a blood disease. Many were terminal.

Most often, when I would find my husband talking to another patient, they would discuss life, family, and work, with only a smattering of the conversation revolving around treatment and diagnosis. They shared a common bond that could not be broken, and they understood the unspoken fears. They learned one another's names and prayed for one another if they did that sort of thing, and many of them did "that sort of thing." They were supportive, cheering one another on when others were discharged while longing for it themselves. Whenever they were readmitted to the ward, they would go room to room looking for "friends." They would be genuinely excited to see them and get caught up in life in their new normal.

Each of James's new roommates would bring new friendships among us all. It seemed so effortless to begin a conversation because we understood the difficulties of the journey. We found that often, as we talked and the friendships blossomed, coffee and snacks would be purchased for the room, not just for an individual. When chemo treatments left a roomie very sick and vulnerable, the others in that room would speak words of encouragement and watch out for them because they understood. It was a beautiful thing to watch and be a part of. There was no comparison on the ward, just an unseen bond among members of this exclusive and unpleasant blood-disease club.

We quickly discovered that the treatments varied as much as the individuals receiving them. When I was asked what kind of chemotherapy James was taking, I could never remember, but neither he nor I cared either. This seemed to be an important detail to remember for some, but my husband and I just wanted it to work. We couldn't care less what it was. During the fifteen-month leukemic fight, James had four different types of chemotherapy, and I only remember the name of the last: Vidaza.

At one point, I remember thinking that they used some rather brutal measures to try to heal people. When he was toward the end of his fight, we found out that his current roommate at the time was receiving a cyanide drip once a week. This young man was barely eighteen years old, and his parents barely left the room. We had a deep ache in our hearts for him, and the bond that went beyond blood disease was formed as we considered how awful this would be if it were one of our precious sons. We would talk with him and his parents, as we encouraged them and they us. We quickly found that neither age nor lifestyle is an indicator of who will get leukemia or a different blood disease. It just happens, and it's horrible.

The comparisons we faced were all outside of the comfort of this strange, isolated, yet comfortable family. All the comparisons we met were outside of the comfort of the fifth floor at the University of Alberta Hospital, and they often came with an intensity that drove home the point that somehow we were doing it wrong.

Many problems surface when you are diagnosed with cancer, one of the most prominent being that so many people have it, had it, or know someone else who had it or has it. You cannot walk an isolated path if this is your diagnosis. Some extraordinary things can also result from this, including the encouragement you can get from those who have traveled the same road. However, you may also find, as we did very quickly, the comparisons were flying!

During the time James was ill, there were several others we knew who also had cancer. Although there were many, I will discuss those I have permission to share, with names omitted and some details changed for the sake of privacy. The three stories I share are of other people, either in our circles or those we met during our own battle. I had lost my own mother to cancer years before, as well as other family members and a spattering of friends and acquaintances. We found we had much support from them. When we sat and talked to these individuals, we realized that not only did each one have a different type of cancer, but they all had very different treatment plans complete with side effects. Some were very optimistic, others not so much. Some chose to keep themselves as busy as possible, while others decided to become more secluded. We were not alone but needed to choose our path, just as they had chosen theirs.

Human beings tend to handle things in various emotional, physical, mental, and spiritual ways. This is partly because we have gone through different life struggles that have helped shape who we are today. These past influences will help determine how we deal with defeat, victory, illness, death, and everything in between. I still believe that in this incredible life experience, we get to have that we are created and formed in the image of God. Because I believe this, I must go one step further and say that He means for us to reveal Him, His character, and His love through these experiences if we allow it to.

One of the things I found so incredibly uplifting and lovely was the massive support we received from the small group of people we knew before cancer and those we found in Ward 5 as well as in the outpatient ward. In this incredible army of fellow soldiers, we found only support, no comparison, just a group of fighters who understood the process. This was a group who was fighting the fight with a "medical cocktail" in one hand and an invisible pom-pom in the other, and they stood at the front line next to us! Beautiful.

One of the individuals we met in the cancer boxing ring decided early on in her diagnosis to go the all-natural route, and she did it with all her might. She believed in it; accepted the outcomes, whatever they would be; and was diligent in her treatments. She wholeheartedly believed that she would be healed and defy the odds. She was supported by those of us fighting alongside her because that was how she decided to fight her battle, and it was none of our business to tell her otherwise. We all understood how hard the struggle is, and so we encouraged her and helped in whatever ways we could. She did so well! She was very positive and utterly dedicated to her regimen. After battling for an extended period well beyond her predicted "expiration date," she succumbed to her disease.

My brother decided to fight his pancreatic cancer by following his oncologist's suggestions as fully as possible, and he was equally as diligent in his efforts to his treatment as anyone else I knew. He decided to try cannabis oil once at the suggestion and persuasion of another and decided that he didn't like it. He never tried anything like it again. We would often go out for dinner with him and his fiancée. During these times, our conversations about what was happening with him and James and how his fiancée and I were handling it all were unreserved, open, honest, and authentic. We got closer than we ever had been, supporting one another. We didn't voice disagreements with some of the decisions made because it wasn't our battle to fight, and the decisions to be made were not ours to make. He also lived past his estimated timeline given by his oncologist and passed away six months after my husband.

Many women of all ages fight breast cancer, and perhaps you are one of them. It is a terrible disease, and regardless of your age, when the diagnosis comes, you will probably find yourself in an emotional tsunami. While receiving treatment, my ever-caring husband, James, would talk to those around him. This was especially true during the hours he was getting chemotherapy treatments, allowing him to share his faith and pray for those around him. One breast cancer patient who was receiving treatment at the same time had young children under the age of ten, and she was very emotional and concerned about her future. Her method of handling her illness was to try as many things as was feasible while listening explicitly to doctors' orders. By undergoing surgery, radiation, chemotherapy, taking high-dose vitamins, and changing her diet entirely, she fought hard, as they all did, with every fiber of her being. She is the lone survivor, and I am also happy to report that the conversations she had with my husband resulted in her praying to accept the Lord.

The questions are not who was right, who did it best, or who did it wrong. The questions are not even which methods, treatments, and outlooks worked best. Honestly, no questions should be brought to the table because they all fought very hard and well! To compare these people's lives and their battles for life with my husband's, which was frequently done, is an injustice to the people in the war and their families. Each person I mentioned tried their best not to worry about what their tomorrows would bring while staying aware of any changes in their conditions, however subtle. The cancers mentioned above were very different; the treatments differed, and the outcomes differed from the onset of each diagnosis.

Factors on How You Can Deal with Your Challenge

It would be a lie if I told you that each person previously mentioned was always cheerful and full of faith because they all, like us, had their occasional struggles. Some of us were prone to giving weekly updates and testimonies of the goodness of God from the front of the church, but that didn't make us more capable in the fight than those who stood and spoke differently during their own painful moments. We quickly learned that all treatments, including homeopathy, can alter a person's moods and thoughts. The potential for depression to creep up on you is one reason you, the patient, must fill out a form each time you visit your oncologist. You may not even be aware that you are beginning to slide into a depression. It is vital to be completely honest about how you are doing physically, emotionally, and psychologically so that your medical providers can help you as early as possible.

WHAT NOT TO SAY

When you have a sickness like cancer, you can find yourself being busier than you may have thought you would be. Things like medications, refills, doctor visits, hospital stays, and, in James's case, blood work three times a week fill your days pretty quickly. But these same things can also tire and weaken you physically, emotionally, and psychologically. Depression is hard to avoid when you are continually told the same bad news on a regular basis, and knowing that all you are doing to keep yourself as healthy as possible is only temporary is difficult not to think about.

It can be easy to stand on the outer rim of someone else's struggle and judge what may look like errors in their judgment or think that they should snap out of a negative, depressed disposition. We have probably all done this; I know I have done this before our adventure, but I quickly learned that it is a very different ball game when you are the one on the playing field.

To be told not to listen to the doctors' advice when they repeatedly tell you they are sorry but it is only a matter of time and that there is nothing they can do, is like telling someone to ignore that their leg is falling off. There are some things you simply cannot ignore, and nor should you! Of course, some may be better at forging their own path in the face of a terminal illness, but I can only speak for us. In doing so, we found that even without talking about it, it took up a fair amount of memory.

In much the same way, being positive will only take you so far. How can you positively share the news like we were given? Remaining hopeful that God could and prayerfully would heal was always in our mouths, hearts, and minds; but so was the continual chatter of the other. Positivity is more of a character trait than it is faith, so being positive doesn't mean you have faith; it just means you are looking for the silver lining in that dark cloud above you. As I have said before, I do believe that God speaks. If we had had a word from Him, our faith would have stood the test, and we would have held on with everything we had. But I had a dream that told a very different story.

For all these reasons, plus a dozen more, at some point, depression may descend on you. Try not to be too hard on yourself if it does. Depression is quite common when you go through a great deal of turmoil and uncertainty, and many medications include side effects like this. In any similar situation, I would suggest that you try to be open to getting the help you need. Self-evaluation can be helpful because no one knows you as well as you do! If you find yourself sleeping more, enjoying less in life, or becoming more irritated, be honest when you see your healthcare worker and speak up.

If you believe in the Christian faith or any other, you will find that your faith will be tested at some point, and it will be a doozy! As a person in ministry, I was not always capable of being what others expected me to be. Yes, I worked full-time outside of the church, but I also led Bible studies, did prayer ministry work, and led prayer meetings. Suddenly, I was not as optimistic as I once was. With the time constraints, I suddenly found myself turning people down for prayer ministry, which was something I was unaccustomed to doing. I was tired, losing hope with every professional conversation we came up against. At this point, I needed to choose more carefully which voices I decided to listen to, and as I pared down my advisers, I realized what a great advantage this was to both James and me.

Another thing that is often overlooked is the duration of your illness or personal challenge and how it directly affects how you manage the ups and downs of not only your emotions but also the trial. It is reasonably easy to be in the above-average range of positivity in the early days of just about anything. However, as you become more tired and the battle continues, it becomes more difficult. As a society, we tend to value and speak well of those who look unscathed by life's hardships, and so we were often applauded in the early days. But as time went on, the criticisms of others began to creep in. Do your best not to get caught in the trap of allowing another person's criticisms of others fighting cancer who don't seem to be doing as well as you are to take you off course. We found in time that these same criticisms came back to us when we became weak, exhausted, and deflated. To those of you outside the cancer boxing ring, please don't judge or criticize what you don't understand. Remember, the duration of the disease seems to erode positivity without notice.

There are many other factors that I haven't touched on, such as individual personalities, family health history, isolation issues, family dynamics, financial pressures, and so much more, that take a toll on your emotional health. Please don't be ashamed if you take a deep dive into sadness or struggle a wee bit as you go through this phase of your life. I speak from personal experience. There is no "getting used" to hearing bad news, especially when it is continually the same bad news. Every time you listen to it, it is a punch in the gut that takes your breath away, leaving you reeling in the face of adversity. Yes, every single time!

How old or young you are, whether you have young children or no children, is also a deciding factor on how you will likely experience and attack your dynamic life shift. Who you have in your corner as your support people and where you are relationally will also play an important role. Whether you are engaged, divorced, happily married, or surrounded by fulfilling life choices will help you determine how you will face your giants. My husband struggled with the thought of leaving his adult kids without his guidance, so I cannot imagine how painful those thoughts would be to grapple with if the children were still young and in the home.

So many things add up to how you fight your battle and attack your problems that there should never be any comparison between those fighting through the same situations. Honestly, what is needed is only compassion, love, and support. Please leave the comparisons outside conversations. We didn't need to hear that we were handling our situation better than others, even though it may have looked that way for a short period. Those same individuals who applauded us during our strong times also condemned us when we succumbed to exhaustion, depletion, resignation, and sadness. None of this was helpful.

You may not understand others' processes and may not like how they are handling them, especially if they are someone you looked up to in the past. Remember, it is not your journey. I can assure you they don't like it either! Please understand they are doing their best, so respect how they have chosen to fight and then fight with them as you help them stand.

The Real Struggle Comes from Within

On this side of the healing journey, and after much contemplation on why these comparisons even occurred, I have come to some conclusions. It seems that comparisons from those outside the inner turmoil bubble (meaning those less touched by the trauma) occur partly because a friend's or family member's illness has altered their world. The problem occurs when they realize it appears to be an impossible situation, issue, or death sentence with no explanation or solution.

It matters little what that situation is, from job losses to fatalities that cause an uncomfortable reality to surface from deep within the recesses of our souls. A question lies in the back of our minds: *Will it happen to me?* This question creates a rift between the safety we believe we have and the possibility of something much less comfortable and appealing. The shift that occurs is from the feeling of invincibility of our youth to the mortality we will all face. It hits us where it hurts, and we must do something with it.

You have heard others say and may have thought it yourself, "It won't happen to me!" But when someone you know is "going through it," this thought is quickly replaced with *Am I next?* This thought can permeate the strongest minds and cause insecurities to rise as we begin to wrestle with death and the reality that life doesn't always go as planned. With these thoughts tucked in the back of our minds, it seems to be very important, and even helpful, to observe those who struggle to determine the best way to handle that crisis if it should also come knocking on our doors.

The criticism can stem from the unspoken and perhaps unrealized thought that if something similar should happen to you, you now know what to do and what not to do because of what you witnessed in the struggle of others. You may be hoping that as you take inner notes, you can walk away with peace that you will do it equally as well or, hopefully, better.

In summary, if we want to bring comfort, strength, and support to others in need, we can best do that by bonding, not comparing. Comparisons are not helpful—ever! When we listen to and support others, we become trusted friends and confidants amid struggle, and it is from this place that suggestions may be made. Remember that we are all made in the image of God. We all have stories, histories, and personalities that are very different from one another. Let's embrace all of it as we walk through the seasons of life together in love and support. After all, we can't look into the future to our difficult season with accuracy, and we will only know how we will do when we get there.

Remember

For those who are supporting,

- Do not compare how you *think* you would handle a crisis against how someone is handling their crisis.
- Do encourage.
- Don't assume that all treatments are the same for each cancer-fighting person. They are not.
- Recognize the emotional struggle of the family and don't dismiss their feelings.

For the caregiver and patient,

- Try to stay as positive as possible.
- Recognize the emotional struggle you are having. Factor in all things that affect how you are doing emotionally, including the duration and severity of your situation.

CHAPTER 5

The Bucket List and the Last Days of Life

My husband and I decided to take a trip to Cleveland, Tennessee, to attend a conference that we had always wanted to attend. The ability to travel this far had come as a massive surprise to us after a bone marrow test showed he had gone into remission, something that was never expected by the medical team. We were shocked and delighted and started planning to tick a few bucket-list items. The things he wanted to do were more extensive than the time we were given to do them. We had been inundated with the constant stream of conversations from various doctors, who all told the same tale with the same unpleasant ending. They had been upfront, and as we sat across from his oncologist, we realized she was as shocked as we were that he was showing normal blast-cell counts. We counted this as a miracle.

She sat and stared at the computer screen with a look of confusion and finally said in a quiet voice, "I can't believe what I am looking at. If it weren't your name at the top of the screen, I would think I was looking at the wrong file. You are in remission. Your blast-cell count is normal!" We were elated! But we were also dumbfounded! The feeling was surreal and not one we had expected to experience. God was so good to us! Talk about ambivalence! Have you ever believed in something for a long time and then been in shock when it finally happened? Well, that was us! We left the doctor's office with her best wishes ringing in our ears, spontaneously packed our bags, and left the following day. We intended to have the best time possible—and we did!

We wanted to share our good news with the army of individuals who had our back, so my entire family went to church the next day, and James took the microphone and told the people that his last bone marrow test had come back showing no cancer. The place erupted in joyous shouts of praise! He received hugs for the first time in eight months, along with many high fives and handshakes, as he, our children, and I cried tears of relief and ecstatic joy. We accepted the news as the healing we had been praying for and expecting, so we planned the much-needed vacation.

Fulfilling bucket-list items is incredibly important if you can fit them into your regimen. Being away from the schedule of appointments can significantly boost your mental health, so don't let anyone talk you out of doing it. This reprieve was incredibly refreshing for James and me as we went from three blood work tests a week, plus transfusions and chemotherapy treatments, to needing to see the doctor once a month! Please take a moment to consider the freedom we had gained! We could have a life again, and we enjoyed every moment of it.

I wish I could say that the trips we went on were without worry, but for me, they were not. Traveling out of the country with a life-threatening diagnosis exempts you from travel insurance, and we knew that the insurance companies would link it to his disease somehow if he got sick or injured. Knowing this, I fought hard to hold on to our breakthrough and freedom, and I tried with everything in me to get rid of the worry. All travel insurance companies turned us down. Despite this, we still chose to go, even though I was much less relaxed than I would have liked. It was a step of faith that I am glad we took.

We had been given three months of bliss, with only two oncologist appointments to attend and blood work twice a month. It felt like heaven! My husband liked to drive, and we did much of that in those three months, going on several day and overnight trips to different places. We traveled to Vancouver and spent a week with our youngest son. Immediately after, we took a drive down the coastal highway for a week in San Francisco. The scenery was magnificent, and the food was fabulous! I must admit that making the trip happen was well worth the expense and my jitters.

From my experiences during this time, I feel bucket-list items should be made and done before you are sick, not while you are sick. I would think that would make them much more enjoyable. If James had not had a period of remission, we would not have been able to check off many, if any, of the things on his wish list because of the constant need for tests and treatments.

It was while we were on our second trip to the United States and toward the end of the three-month mark that I began to notice subtle changes in my husband's appearance and energy levels. True to himself, he never said a word, but it became very evident a day or two before we were to travel home at the end of May that something wasn't right. I became concerned, but he assured me he was fine, while his usual quiet demeanor became even more subdued. He was also aware that the tides of health were turning. Within forty-eight hours of our return home, blood test results told us the truth we didn't want to hear. The leukemia was back, and it was more aggressive than ever. The hours spent in the University of Alberta Hospital's outpatient unit became longer, as did the number of days we were there. Sometimes, it totaled up to fourteen hours per day, five days a week. Once again, the stress began to build as his health rapidly deteriorated.

It was at this time that I began to lean heavily on those people I had designated to be my "voices" to spread prayer requests and updates. I think I still went to church most Sundays, although I can't completely remember. James spent a lot of time in and out of the hospital. It was also at this time that the recurrence of unnecessary, unhelpful, and hurtful things began to surface with more clarity, opportunity, and severity than it had in the past.

Please Refrain from Saying "Where Is Your Faith? Do You Believe He Was Healed?"

In the last three months, the questions "Where is your faith?" and "Don't you believe he was healed?" came at us more often than we would have liked. These were such frustrating questions because they left us with a mix of depletion and stirred hope. The trouble with navigating hope and faith is that when things look like they are going one way, there is that undeniable and unwelcome sharp left turn that leaves you gasping for air. What did we do when we lost our footing momentarily? We prayed, we believed, we had communion, and we called the elders to come and pray.

But then again, there was that dream. What was I supposed to do with that? The answer to the above questions was that, yes, of course, we believed he had been healed. We had acted on that by going on holidays, renewing his passport for ten years, and began planning some household renovations. Did we doubt he was healed? No. Were we cautious? Absolutely! Did our feet feel like they were on unstable ground? Definitely yes!

I do wish there was some way I could adequately explain to you how this felt for us, but I am at a loss for words. To hear the words "You have cancer" is hard enough to handle. At that point, you will likely find yourself in shock but with the strength to fight and the drive to do everything and anything in the hope of a positive outcome. However, when you have been fighting through countless days of feeling ill, with as many numerous adverse reports, it tends to wear you out. But this!

These words were a kick to the gut! The words hit me with tremendous force because James and I were depleted. We had nothing more to give to this fight. Once again, I was afraid!

It was during this time that we needed the faith of others to hold us up. I wanted to shout, "Pray and believe *for* us, please. We cannot do it ourselves," but the words didn't come. I couldn't form them in my mouth, even though it was the desperate cry of my heart. I wanted to tell those around me that it was their faith now that could move our mountains (Mark 11:23–24), and where two or three are gathered in His name (Matthew 18:20), there He is in the midst of them, ready to answer requests. James and I were so battle weary that we needed to rest on the sidelines, and we were humble enough to acknowledge it to our closest friends.

We appreciate so much those who prayed fervently for us during this time. But I must also add that there were others who put the responsibility for James's healing almost entirely upon us. I had no words to explain that I could no longer do it! It wasn't that I didn't want to fight. I just could not fight any longer. I had no more strength inside of me for war, and James had even less.

How do you tell people that you believe things will turn out differently than what the congregation of faith is telling you? At what point do you resign yourself to the will of God and surrender a life you love to the destiny that you believe God foretold? How do you explain to people that you had a dream before the illness came where you understood that your husband was going to die while holding on to faith for his healing at the same time? There were no words!

I found myself crying out in a tug-of-war between my willingness to surrender to a future I did not think I could bear and the pressure to manipulate the hand of God to do something other than His will. And so, my heart, mind, and soul cried, "If possible, may this situation be taken away from me. Yet, not what I want, but what you want"(Luke 22:42). I was learning to trust God in a way I never thought I would have to. I was learning to lean on promises I had not fully comprehended before this moment, all because I had run out of strength for the final battle.

We had been told many times by doctors that he would die, and we had been told just as many times that he would not reach remission. Except he did go into remission! We began to understand that there are no easy answers to life and death. I wish there were. It would be great if healing or the preferred outcome happened every time for every person in need. But it doesn't. We were encouraged to continue to confess that he was healed and not to back down and let death win. We were told that this was just a test and that he would be completely healed if we would not give in to the diagnosis and the things we had been told. Maybe all this is true, and perhaps we missed the most incredible miracle and testimony of our lives, but James and I also learned some things along the way. We learned that every question asked came with an answer that can only be given in the middle of trials. I will present some of those questions and answers in the following pages.

Does He (God) Have Authority over All Things? Can He Heal?

Even as I type these words, I know the answer. The short and simple answer is yes, absolutely! However, just like in so many areas of life, there are things within this statement that are up to us to discover and settle as a fact of faith in our hearts. Some of the events we go through cause a shift in our thinking, and that shift can cause us to grapple with coming to terms with trusting God as we lean into Him in faith and accept His designs, whatever they may be.

For us, this occurred in the resurgence of cancer after remission, which was an even more aggressive acute myeloid leukemia. The first round had been aggressive enough to cause the doctors to make him a case study. Now, it seemed to have a mind of its own. However, this turn of events caused an awkwardness to develop in our relationships and friendships that carried on until well after his death.

There were many causes for this awkward and stifling shift. I was the first among my friends to be losing a spouse, so no one knew what to do with me. What do you say in the face of such devastation at such a young age? Do you comfort? Console? Encourage? Challenge? Empathize? Grieve? Give up? Or do you push forward in your thinking and believe in healing? Emotionally, I was all over the place as well. I didn't always know what I needed, and what I needed yesterday was not what I hoped for today. I was a mess, and no one knew how to approach me or what to say to me either. However, the pressure I felt from those around me to ignore my husband's condition was not what I needed.

Our family was less optimistic, energetic, and full of faith than we had been initially. We had been challenged in our faith. Originally, we stood up and took the challenge boldly and courageously, but now we found ourselves wrestling with that very concept of faith. Where we had been unwavering and declarative months before, we found ourselves no longer capable of being courageous or willing to say that we believed he would live.

Perhaps we were wavering, but then there was that disturbing dream I had had. We may have shifted from the mindset of denial to reality. But who likes the truth and reality we were faced with? Certainly not us. Maybe we wavered because we were depleted emotionally and spiritually. We were physically and mentally exhausted. Were we excusing our lack of faith and hope for something better to happen, or were we taking the hand of the one walking us through the valley of the shadow of death? There were so many questions. I don't expect to know the answers to these questions anytime soon.

The people around us wondered where my faith had gone in the past twelve to fifteen months. In reality, I still believed, and so did my family. I still had hope, and so did my family. We all still trusted God. The difference was that, at this point, I trusted God for His plans and purposes to be done. I did not push my will and desire into an uncertain future. I had come to the end of my will for this to go my way. I had lost belief in my perception of who God is, as well as the faith in myself and my magnificent prayers to convince God to move my mountains.

I abandoned what I thought to be true and began to realize that trusting God meant that God and God alone rules the earth and is the author of life and death. Throughout the grueling fifteen months, I realized that we all have a certain number of days to live and that I don't dictate to God Almighty, creator of heaven and earth, what to do. I don't tell him how long someone should be allowed to live. In short, I realized I have no right to tell God how to do His job! I began to let Him do in me, my circumstances, and my family whatever it was He wanted to do.

The shift was not pleasant, but it was good. I began to feel more secure, in many ways, including in my faith, than I had in a long time because I was no longer striving for something I wanted to happen. Instead, I began resting on His abilities to carry me or us regardless of how things turned out. I began to trust His judgments, plans, and purposes for us all.

Don't get me wrong. I didn't want my husband to die; but I had come to realize that I couldn't work hard enough, pray long enough, quote enough scriptures, or declare enough decrees to make it happen. I needed to trust God. I needed to trust God for who He is, not what He can do for me! Eventually, I came to understand that I cannot dare risk the chance of "twisting the arm of God" to get what I want. I had learned to trust Him, even if James died. This was a very tough thing to learn.

I don't know you or your circumstances or convictions, so your walk will be different than mine in many ways, but it may carry some of the same challenges mine did. You may have a completely different set of beliefs or no beliefs at all. Regardless of your situation or faith, reconciling yourself to the inevitable death of a loved one is incredibly difficult. You may feel more silenced now than you have at any point in your life before this. You may also feel deeply that the only ones who seem to really "get it" are the few rare souls who have walked a mile or two in your shoes.

I want you to know that you will make it through this time of turmoil. Don't become discouraged to the point of throwing your hands up in the air and walking away from hope for the miraculous or the truth that God loves and cares deeply for you when you come to this crossroads. You may not be able to control or dictate the circumstances, events, or people around you; but there is one thing you do have some control over, and that is you! There may be times when you are frustrated at the medical system, but you do not need to lash out. You may find that you have had enough of unhelpful comments from voices without experience, but you do not need to lash out.

You get to decide when you wake up in the morning how full or empty your glass will be. You get to choose if you allow the circumstances and the heaviness to control you. You decide when you rise and fight, if you will pray or not, or if you will be thankful for the events the day holds. You can choose what you will continually think about. And then, you get to decide what you will release to Him. He is the One who ultimately holds your future and the future of your loved ones in His capable hands.

At this point, six years after James's death, I will say I did not do everything as well as I could have. I admit that there were many times I felt annoyed and even irritated, and there were some people I did respond to in a way that was not as controlled as I suggest in this writing or as well as I would have liked. I ask that for those with whom I was rude, please forgive me.

When we found ourselves at the end of our cancer journey, we reflected on the many ups and downs and multiple twists and turns that had taken place. We acknowledged that the emotional roller coaster we had endured reflected each and every one of these. But we also needed to recognize that we had gained a bank filled with information we would rather not have learned about a disease we did not think we would ever face, but we did make it through. We found ourselves here, at the end of his life, whether we wanted to or not.

When he was admitted for the last time, I spent every day and night with him in the hospital until his days were over. I watched him take his final breath at 1:09 a.m. on Saturday, September 9, 2017.

Remember

- If you pray, pray for others when they are running low on faith, strength, and hope.
- Don't put added pressure on those during the possible end. Remember, they are battle weary.
- Do not tell those who are struggling that it is their fault that things are not turning around.
- There are no easy answers to life and death.
- Trust God for His plans and purposes in everything you go through, whether you understand it or not.
- You decide each day what you will focus on and if you will look for the positives or settle on the negatives.

CHAPTER 6

Healthcare Providers

Recently, I talked with a woman from my community who has stage four cancer. She found herself troubled by the visit and lack of care she received from her home care worker. She recently had surgery, and the follow-up appointments had been scheduled in her home. Although this had been going on for several weeks, she found herself with a different aide than usual. It did not go well. Upon arrival, the healthcare worker admitted that she had not had time to read the medical report and wasn't sure what needed to happen. I understand how this could happen in their profession, but it might have been wiser if she had not mentioned it. It significantly diminished the patient's confidence in the care received.

As I write this chapter, I want you to know that healthcare workers are an asset to their profession and should be treated with the utmost respect. What I am stating is my opinion and not a smear campaign to discolor the reputation of a much-needed industry. It is only to shine a little helpful light on something that tends to be noticed and discussed but does not help those struggling when it seems to go awry. So bear with me as I attempt to address this issue gently and respectfully.

While James was ill, we got to know the nurses in the outpatient ward reasonably well and found them lovely, caring, sensitive, and accommodating. The nurse practitioner initially in charge when we began our visits was a tremendous asset and exceptional at her job. She was very hands-on. She would take the time to visit each patient every time they were in, and we appreciated her so much. What this did was help her to get to know the people, and consequently, she would often catch an underlying health concern that went unnoticed by the inexperienced eye (mostly mine and James's). Very often, the things she noticed were subtle changes, but she would order testing and find that there was, indeed, something brewing. As I said, she was an exceptional woman who did an outstanding job! It was a sad day when she left after being offered a position elsewhere. She deserved her promotion. She was a tremendous asset as the head of the outpatient ward, leaving an incredible void.

Perhaps we had our sights set a little high because of the initial level of care and concern we were shown, but then again, our expectations may have set us up to be disappointed in her replacement's abilities amid my husband's deterioration. She was very different than her former colleague. Where the previous one had been personally attentive, this one was more file and document-focused. Neither is necessarily more wrong or right, just different.

You may find that you have both great and not-so-great experiences as you find yourself needing their expertise. There are doctors, nurses, nurses' aides, and many others who feel that their life's calling is to work in healthcare. These people will often go above and beyond on any workday. You can see the concern and compassion in their eyes, and they can be trusted to do the best for you even when it is inconvenient for them. They take their jobs seriously, love their work, and honestly care about their patients; the list of these individuals would be too long to write down if I could remember their names. When we entered the fight of our lives, we went into the ring expecting a high level of care from each health care professional we were in contact with, but it was not always the case.

I am not a person who looks at another profession, especially this one, as if they cannot be trusted. I choose to believe that the vast majority are doing what they do because they are drawn to care for those in need. I believe they want to help and love to be a bright spot in someone else's day. I have accepted that most of them are in their field because they love what they do and not for any other reason. Having said that, they are also human, and as human beings, we all have days where we are not in the best of moods. I also recognize that they, like the rest of us, can make mistakes.

I recognize that this is a tricky topic, and I want to move through it from the only vantage point I have: being a caregiver. I have friends who are nurses and others who hold various positions in the medical community. As I spoke with many of them, I found that if or when they have made an error, they have openly accepted and taken responsibility for it. None of the people I know has ever shrugged off an error they made as if it didn't matter. Each of them was tough on themselves for any mistakes they had made, and it didn't get easier to handle the longer they did the job. To be completely honest, each person we were in contact with was careful and watchful as they worked, and I stress that we should appreciate every one of them.

You may wonder why I need to bring this up while discussing what not to say. My many reasons stem from a heart deeply grateful for those in the medical community who have walked with us. We would have lost James had it not been for the excellent care we received within the first few days after he was initially diagnosed and admitted, in addition to the many months before his passing. The care was consistent, sincere, and prompt. They were a fantastic group of individuals.

However, one of the continually surfaced conversations revolved around the antimedical profession viewpoint, which is why I feel the need to address it in this book. I don't have all the answers, and I would like you to know that I also appreciate natural, homeopathic care as much as I do the more well-known medical profession. What I do want to do is give honor and respect to those who are so selfless so often. Even though we may not approve or appreciate all the practices of any profession, we must give credit where it is due.

Let me say that I absolutely believe in health! There are some things we should be doing to achieve the best level of health for ourselves. Four aspects are critical to our overall well-being:

- Healthy living
- Exercise
- Regular dental and doctor checkups
- Mental health wellness

What I am saying is that we cannot put complete responsibility on the professionals.

If we are going to improve our long-term health, the first thing we must do is take some responsibility for ourselves. Doing as much as possible, regardless of where you are in your health journey, is a step in the right direction because you will feel better for it. Eating properly is one of the best things we can do for our minds and bodies. I admit that this isn't always easy to do in our society. I have been as guilty as anybody else, especially during the fifteen months of James's illness. Wendy's and Tim Hortons were just across the street from the hospital and were the views we often had from his room, so let's talk about needing a coffee and a donut or a burger and fries for dinner.

Sometimes, a fast-food burger and fries are the easiest way to go when you are out and about ticking off the to-do list while running out of time. Getting together with friends at your favorite eatery is a North American privilege that we all love to indulge in on occasion, and who doesn't like to go out for a meal that you did not prepare? The reality is many of us eat out too often, and as someone with a background in the food industry, I know that the food prepared in restaurants could be better for you. They are often packed with preservatives and high in calories with added sugar to make them taste better, but we fill our bellies with them without the benefits. The other reality is that we often don't like the taste of the healthier food option, but getting used to the flavor and texture may be worth it.

Exercise is another area we avoid because it is time-consuming, challenging, and often painful! Once again, we know that it is worth it. Not only will we look better, but we will also feel better. If you have ever been a person who has frequented the gym, run track, or hiked regularly, you know that there are few things more satisfying than the feeling you have after a good workout, sore or not. Not only does your body feel better, but it also works for the better. But the benefits don't end there because your mental and emotional health will also perk up. Do what you can, and do what you enjoy. Take up hiking, long walks, weights, or some other form of exercise. If you work within your abilities, you will reap the benefits.

Regular checkups with your doctor are invaluable because they can prevent or treat many potential issues that can cause serious health issues over time. We are often unaware of some things that may be happening with our bodies because we feel fine. But if you do have something brewing and you go for your yearly medical or dental checkup, your doctor may be able to catch it early enough to implement treatment options that don't include long-term medications. Regular checkups also provide you and your doctor with a roadmap of your health history, which will only help you and your doctor as you age.

I am blessed to have an excellent family practitioner willing to work with my homeopath to keep my health as optimal as possible. Although this hasn't always been the case, today, more and more MDs are willing to work closely with natural care practitioners. If yours doesn't, and this is a route you are interested in, do some research to find one who will.

Another area that has recently begun to get more attention is that of our mental health. Past traumas are worth resolving because they can significantly affect our overall health. It is true! Research shows that the more childhood traumas one has, the more likely one's health will show it. Some, perhaps even many, diseases can be linked to unresolved wounds and ensuing emotions we have been unwilling to deal with.

As you can see, our overall health comes from a wide variety of areas and cannot or should not be left up to the medical professionals to correct. Overall, we are responsible for at least some of the contributing factors. Remember, we each need to ask ourselves, "Am I doing all I can to live my best health?" Yes, it can be costly, time-consuming, and uncomfortable. Yes, it can feel invasive! But when we look at our health over our entire existence, can we not accept at least some of the responsibility? It could then become a journey that pays well in the long run.

Having said all this, I want to assure you that I also understand that ill health, diseases, and cancer can happen to us at any time, even if we are doing all we can to be healthy. I understand that we can be born with a predisposition to a particular issue or even be born with the disease itself, having done nothing to warrant that disease in the first place. Once again, the looming question could be "Why do babies get cancer?" I do not know. What I do know, and what I believe, is that we should accept the help given to us by those who provide it while we work daily to improve our overall health.

Please Refrain from Saying "Medical Professionals Do Not Care"

I have said all this to lead into this part of the conversation. This may surprise some of you, but while my husband was ill, some accused the doctors and nurses of not caring about us. Unfortunately, this happened repeatedly from a handful of individuals. One accusation was that the doctors, especially the oncologists, only cared about the money they were making off his disease. They conversed with us and gave us CDs to watch that discouraged the use of medical interventions. These conversations quickly became an agitation to us and were anything but helpful.

Our perspective was very, very different. Never once did we feel like the oncologist did not care. The nurses were phenomenal, and our family doctor is one of the best. The doctor we met on the night of my husband's initial admission on June 4, 2016, stayed well past her shift hours to meet with us. She was kind, gentle, and compassionate, even after midnight! When we were finally admitted to the room, the nurses were super attentive, and the head nurse also stayed extra hours after her shift to ensure he was stable. The oncologist was involved in every aspect of his care. What I am trying to say is this: we felt cared for by 99 percent of everyone we came in contact with. We did not need to have doubts planted in our minds that the people working with us were actually out to kill us. This thought process cannot be helpful.

By bringing an accusation like this to a conversation with someone struggling with health issues, you rob them of the trust they need in those taking care of them. When you get into an airplane, you cannot question the integrity of your pilot to get you to your destination by believing he has ulterior motives; he is secretly hoping the plane crashes while he parachutes to the ground in safety. That would be ludicrous and counterproductive. So why would you plant this thought into the mind of someone regarding their specialist, oncologist, or other healthcare provider?

There comes a time when you have to trust. Can you believe that they are working toward finding a solution for the problem at hand? It isn't uncommon to be unsure about the procedures or medications being prescribed, but when you feel that way, ask questions until you are satisfied. If you still feel uncertain, you have the right to get a second opinion, so exercise your rights to do so. But once again, I say this: don't plant fear or doubt in the minds of those fighting.

I was told by a man that a person should never go the medical route unless they absolutely had to, for example, if they needed immediate lifesaving needs or had broken bones. My fundamental question would be "Why would they try to save your life then and not at other times?" If we are going to have this conversation, I think we should look at it logically overall. When you plant doubt, you can unknowingly encourage irrational, harmful, and costly actions. Comments like these can cause someone to delay treatment. By the time a decision is made to follow doctors' orders, there is little they can do to restore health.

We found through this walk that most doctors and nurses are open to listening to your concerns and discussing any issues you have. With that in mind, if you feel at any time that you are not being heard or are being dismissed, please speak up, but do not say that they do not care. When James was in the final days of his life, one of the nurses came in to give him a pain injection and began sobbing because he was unconscious and at the end of his life. As each nurse on the floor who had cared for him over the last months came in to see us and say their goodbyes, many were emotional. I assure you they do care!

What Do You Do with Those Who Seem to Give Less-than-Adequate Care?

I should clarify why I feel the need to add this next segment. It is not because I am disgruntled or angry or desire to cause harm to anyone. But I also acknowledge that, at times, professional people do not respond the way we would most like them to. Unfortunately, there are times when things do get overlooked. I will preface what I will say with the comment that I believe nothing that happened was intended to harm James. I also acknowledge that they were doing what they felt was the correct thing to do at the time.

As my husband's illness progressed, the level of care he continued to receive remained consistent. We were satisfied and felt we were being seen, heard, and cared for in the best way possible. We did have a few challenges along the way, and although I won't go into detail, I will summarize the ugly and unhelpful incidents briefly.

When my husband began to have more health crises at the end of July 2017, we found ourselves rushing to the emergency after midnight with him in severe pain. Unsure if he was having another heart attack, we quickly responded and hoped for the same quality of care we had been accustomed to. The triage nurse promptly got him a bed, and other nurses began to fill the room. One of the nurses started asking him about his health history, which, by this time, was becoming extensive. He started with his previous heart attack. As he rattled off his history, one of the nurses blurted out, "That's great! Is there anything else you would like to diagnose yourself with?"

Dumbfounded by her response, he remained silent. I, however, would not allow this comment to remain unanswered. I was kind but firm when I said, "He is not diagnosing himself. You asked for a health history. That is what he is giving you. Perhaps you shouldn't have asked the question if you weren't prepared for the answer." In my frustration, exhaustion, and mental fog, I then replied with a comment that didn't need to be said, revealing my irritation. "A little less attitude from you would be greatly appreciated!" Understandably, she was angry and silent when she left the room. I upset her with my response. I admit I should have held my tongue by not replying with the last bit of verbiage.

The last nurse practitioner we had, whom I previously mentioned, seemed to be a continual thorn in my side. Much too often, it seemed like I was asking her to come and assess his condition or a problematic new symptom. In my opinion, she spent a lot of time in her office, had very little interaction with the patients, and didn't seem interested in getting to know the people behind the files she looked at. When my husband began having headaches (which can mean a brain bleed in leukemia patients), she came and visually looked at him at our request. She didn't send him for any tests or blood work and didn't call his oncologist. From her visual assessment and a few questions, she concluded that he was dehydrated and constipated.

I was dumbfounded. About three days later, with the headache increasing in intensity, she requested an X-ray so she could see how constipated he was. I jumped on the opportunity to ask that an X-ray of his head be done as well but was denied. I pursued my request with many reasons why I felt it should be done. I was denied.

I requested she speak with his oncologist. I was denied. This merry-go-round of a conversation went on for about two weeks, with each request I made being denied. It turned out the headache resulted from the suspected brain bleed, and had an X-ray been done when first requested, there might have been something that could have been done. I was angry about this for many months after his death and felt he had been cheated out of more life.

I discussed my frustration with my family, and it was determined that I should share my concern with the staff caring for him during his end of life. As I did so, I was relieved to find that they were neither upset with me nor did they run to protect one of their own. Upon verifying my story, they began the process needed to address it. These people care! They are not pretending, so please do not rob someone else of the assurance that they won't be taken care of because of your medical fears.

The best advice I can give those of you walking through this minefield is this: always be aware of what is happening, do your best, and trust God. Try not to allow the opinions of others to dictate how you proceed with your medical team. It may be essential to remember that we live in a society that can have extreme views on a variety of things, and our healthcare is one of them. Is it because we can practice critical thinking that we tend to have some trust issues? But that doesn't mean our doctors and nurses are out to kill us. Have faith in God and trust that His hand is on you and on those He has placed over you. As a side note, if you choose to go the natural health route, it is critically important that you have a homeopathic doctor because herbal medicines are medicines. If you have anything life-threatening, this professional will be able to prescribe your best homeopathic cocktail for your specific condition.

God forbid, if you find yourself in a similar situation to mine, speak up earlier rather than later. Don't be timid when you are caring for your loved one; but in the end, even if something should go awry, forgive.

Forgiveness is a huge factor in moving into emotional healing. Without it, we can find ourselves stuck in anger. Forgiveness helps us move through the grief process. I admit I took this incident to heart for longer than I should have, and I knew it. One day, two friends and I decided to put it to rest once and for all. After a few hours of conversation, prayers, and tears, I was able to forgive completely, release her, and accept that he was in the last days of his life when this occurred. How many more days he might have lived if the circumstances were different wouldn't have been that many or that lovely, perhaps only a week or two. But I had wanted every precious day to cherish with him, so I would have gladly taken them.

Forgiveness when there has been a medical error can be complicated to achieve, and as I said, I struggled with it for a while. I needed prayer and counseling to finally release the nurse practitioner. I blamed her for James's death. In accusing her, I allowed bitterness to take root in my heart, even though I had said I had forgiven her. Did I have a right to be angry? Perhaps? But holding on to it was only hurting me in the long run.

In fifteen months, these were the only two scenarios out of countless appointments, exams, and hospital stays where I felt we were not heard or given adequate care. Your team of medical professionals does care for you, so be kind to them.

Remember that God holds the number of our days on Earth, and if we have done all we can in faith, then it is time to trust Him with our future and the future of our loved ones. He knows the number of hairs on our heads and our every step, so can we trust Him as the author of life and death? He does not make mistakes!

Remember

- Don't criticize the medical field.
- Do what you can to maintain good health.
- Eat a good diet, exercise, get regular checkups, and work on your past.
- Don't tell someone their doctor is only in it for the money.
- Don't tell someone that it was a mistake to go to their family physician.
- Don't tell someone that their doctor is withholding information from them.
- Don't rob someone of trust in the doctors and nurses caring for them.

CHAPTER 7

Celebrations of Life

I came home from the hospital in the dawning hours of Saturday, 9, 2017. I couldn't sleep as the events of the night before began to replay in my mind, which would eventually cut a permanent rut. I was home but still immersed in the final hours of James's life. It was over! I couldn't believe it! I was in shock. I was deeply aware that he was gone but was unable to accept that it had actually happened. This was the first day of my life as a widow. A widow! That word seemed so strange to me—so foreign, cold, and unlovely.

When my son, daughter-in-law, and I left the hospital, we were given a folder and asked, "Where do you want the body sent?" I looked at the folder that said What to Do Next. It was blue. "Where did we want the *body* sent?" The nurses on staff were compassionate and gentle. But that question—that *body* was my husband! A body? I don't remember anything else as I took the blue folder and walked out of Ward 5H at the U of A Hospital for the last time.

This was the beginning of many, many months of countless responses from people who stopped me dead in my tracks with my mouth hanging open. I don't want you to think that there were never any good things said or done because there were many. I knew the nurses at the hospital were only doing their jobs, and they were asking questions they needed answered. It was just that it seemed so strange to hear my husband being referred to as a body.

Many times, the questions that came my way needed to be asked, and many of them kept me from getting lost in the unpredictability of emotions I felt. As I have said before, grief is hard. I quickly lost my appetite and found nothing looked, smelled, or tasted appealing. For the first time in decades, I no longer wanted to cook. I began to lose weight, and others began to notice. I was thankful when a few of these friends started checking up on me to ensure I was eating. A simple yes was insufficient; they wanted to know exactly what I was eating and what I had eaten that day. I was living on fried egg sandwiches, toast with peanut butter and honey, or pasta with sauce from a jar. I would nibble away at what I had made but throw most of it away. I dreaded the kitchen, the food, the preparation, and the cleanup, so I avoided spending time in it. Most days, I wasn't feeling well physically.

It may seem odd, but simple, caring comments about my diet coming from friends were not invasive but helpful to me. I spent about three months not eating well, not eating much, and losing about twenty pounds. My kids became worried and signed me up for a packaged meal kit that came right to my door. This was a good decision on their part and very helpful for me, and it got me back in the kitchen cooking meals. As my diet improved, the sandwiches became less of a staple.

I didn't need to be asked if I had showered during the week or if I was taking care of my personal hygiene because I found the tub a place of relaxation and refuge. I understood my friends were concerned about me, and although there were days I was annoyed to hear them calling me yet again to ask the same old questions, it did help me from getting lost in my emotions.

As I did, you may find that simple everyday tasks can feel burdensome, and you may find that you are uninterested in doing any of them.

You may push yourself to do them, or you may avoid them. I'm not sure there is a right way to do this except to do what you can. We need to eat. Food delivery services were beneficial, and surprisingly, the food was good. But remember, you will need time to rest and recover, so give yourself the time to do so.

It seemed like almost immediately after I left the hospital, my mind began to turn to mush. I began to realize that "grief brain" is real! I found that if I wrote things down, I would get things done; if I didn't, I would never remember what needed doing. It may seem silly, but this list included simple things like sweeping the floor, taking out the garbage, and getting a little exercise. I had another list of tasks that needed extra stamina and mental preparation, like going to the funeral home, sending off death certificates, and meeting with the life insurance agent.

Thank goodness for good friends who immediately jumped in and helped to steer me through the clutter of decisions and preparations that needed to be made. They refused to let me go to the funeral home alone and even checked to make sure the funeral home had received the "right body." This may sound silly, but it was a genuine fear I had, and one I could not talk myself out of, even after the funeral director had assured me they were certain they had. I knew it was an irrational fear, but I seemed unable to steer around it at the time. These longtime friends stepped in and made sure my worries could be put to rest, and they did it without making me feel irrational or incapable.

I was so thankful that my husband had prearranged his funeral, even though it felt very odd and sort of morbid when we went to do it. He didn't want to plan it but also didn't want to put pressure on me and the kids to have to do it. He had most of the details completed when he passed, but there were still things I needed to make decisions on. Some of those things included who would do the catering and what would be served. I recognize that these were not difficult questions on an average day, but for me, they were suddenly mind-boggling and felt heavy with responsibility.

Why were there so many decisions? I didn't care what we ate at the reception! But the one question that was the most annoying was whether I knew how many people would be coming to the funeral. How was I supposed to know? Unlike a wedding, you don't ask for an RSVP. You send out the news, and people either show up or don't. My brain was overloaded, overwhelmed, and exhausted from all the months before. Once again, I was so thankful I did not have to make all these decisions alone.

Every person handles and processes the days leading up to the funeral differently. It was not something I wanted to do. There was absolutely nothing about the day that I was looking forward to. Phone calls and texts were coming in from friends and family wanting details, directions to the funeral home, and hotel information. Thank god for social media! I could post much of this information on my page, so it handled many of those questions.

Time has a way of continuing onward, with or without your willingness or preparedness. I woke up the day of the funeral and heard myself say aloud "I don't want to do this. I really, really, really don't want to do this" countless times as I prepared myself for the day. My children looked at me many times and hugged me as the tears flowed freely down my face. The day had come, and there was nothing I could do about it and no way to stop it.

Unfortunately, the celebration of life, or funeral as it used to be called, deserves its own special place in this book. It is the day when you will see the most people for the longest amount of time and be in the worst emotional state to handle it. It is also in this place that you will find yourself unprepared for many of the conversations you will have. In this concentrated environment, the floor is open for the waves of people wanting to give their condolences and "helpful tokens of advice." It is this combination of events that provided the most opportunity for examples of what not to say.

The funeral home was excellent when I arrived with my children and in-laws. I felt distanced—almost separated—from the events playing out. I realize now that shock was still propelling me forward.

It seemed that people began arriving very soon afterward. I still didn't want to be doing this. Somehow, that made the time fly. Two of my brothers were among the first to arrive. They had come to be a shield to me and redirect people when I had had enough. I was so thankful for them on that day as they stood at the doorway to the "family room," waiting for me to say I had had enough.

It is safe to say that almost every person who comes to the celebration will be affected and emotional to some degree or another. For at least an hour or more, these people will be in an atmosphere of remembrance of a person they had a relationship with or in support of a family member they care about. People who attend will hurt for you, and they will inevitably want to say or do something to ease your pain.

Please Refrain from Saying "You Seem to Be Taking This Very Well" and "You Knew It Was Coming"

Two statements that were said by more than one person at the celebration of life were "You seem to be taking this very well" and "You knew it was coming." These two phrases are like bookend statements. They hold between them thoughts and unspoken expectations on how you should be responding during your public grieving or just grieving, in general. It is almost like everything in the middle of these two sentences is how you should be responding, while the bookends of "You seem to be handling this very well" and "You knew he was going to die" are where you don't want to be. Trust me. You don't!

You Seem to Be Taking This Very Well

After the funeral, as we entered the reception hall for the tea, the stream of people who wanted my ear seemed endless. The funeral was very well attended, and I hadn't reached the reception hall door before the first individual stopped me. Most of the conversations were respectful, kind, and warmly received. There always seemed to be a family member close by, such as one of my sons, a brother, my father-in-law, or a close friend for emotional support. Once again, to every one of you, I appreciated this immensely.

Although I had cried many tears at the house, I had not cried at the funeral. It was a hard day. I am a crisis person, which means I handle difficult and unpleasant moments by being in control. I was pushing through when there it was: "You seem to be taking this very well!"

I just stood and stared at the person talking to me like they spoke a foreign language. I was struggling with understanding what they had said. Did it mean the way it sounded or not? Was I doing it wrong already? How am I supposed to be doing this? I had never buried a husband before, and I remember standing there rethinking what had been said. Had I misheard or misinterpreted, or was I just unable to process the conversation? I didn't know how to respond, and I don't think I did. I stood and stared at them without uttering a word. They continued speaking, but I remember nothing else of what they said.

I suggested earlier that people often watch you for your responses, hoping to find something they can carry with them that may be helpful if they go through something similar. Although it may feel like it, you are unlikely to be judged for doing "it" wrong.

Honestly, from my heart, I want to let you know that how an individual looks during a difficult time or event may not be a true indication of how they are truly doing emotionally. On the day of the funeral, I could "buck it up" and do what needed to be done because I was mentally prepared to do it. Emotionally, however, I was very unprepared for many things that were said. Coping the way I do protects me from greater emotional pain and sorrow that I didn't have the capacity to feel or deal with at the time.

To help you better understand what I am conveying here, I will say that there is an element of shock that is still very real in the first week or two after the death of a loved one. Preparing for the funeral takes time and can remove focus from dealing with the reality of the loss until after the day has passed. Shock is a buffer to the intensity of emotion that needs to be released, but make no mistake, that release will come. For some people, the waves of reality and emotion will come as the funeral solidifies your loss. For others, it will happen over a more extended time.

The funeral, however, is not the place to comment or suggest whatever "you seem to be taking this very well" was meant to imply. I was doing fine because I was wrapped up in my self-protecting coping mechanism, but I was also not doing fine. What was I doing? I was doing what was expected of me because I was James's wife, and I loved him deeply. I think I would have made him proud that day. In addition, I relied heavily on Jesus to get me through the day. However, the next days and months would tell a different story because the shock would not last forever.

Anticipatory Grief

I want to share a brief segment on anticipatory grief from my personal perspective. When others would mention that I knew he was going to die, the insinuation was that my grief should be lessened because I knew it was coming. But there is a huge difference between grief and anticipatory grief, or the anticipation and knowledge that someone will die.

Anticipatory grief is the time when the heart and emotions of those facing a loss begin to prepare for the imminent grief that they will, unfortunately, have to experience. As a side note, this doesn't only include the losses of people you love, although it often does. It can also include any other massive life shift, including the final signing of the divorce documents or the end of a career.

Anticipating the loss of a loved one whose prognosis is terminal is not the same as having lost them. Nothing can prepare you for that. Anticipatory grief happens much more in the mind than in the heart as you consider what your life will be like without the one you love. It is difficult as you watch them deteriorate and weaken, but you also know it is part of the process. During the waning process, you will expect death and will therefore grieve before their end because you are waiting for the day to come.

You will grieve with them for everything they have lost the ability to do until you eventually reach the final stages, where you hope they will pass away easily and quickly. You will come to the place where you ache for the suffering to stop, the pain to go away, and death to come. Anticipatory grief is the process of beginning to let go. It isn't easy. It can, but it often does not make the loss easier to handle.

Grief, on the other hand, is the harsh reality of the expected death. The impact of the actual loss of my husband was both overwhelming and unexpected, even though I knew it was imminent. I had known it would happen, and I had grieved many things in anticipation of his passing, and yet I found that none of the things I thought about or felt beforehand prepared me for this moment. Not only did I have the months before to "prepare" myself for his death, but I had also had the dream months before where the Lord Himself had spoken. I knew it was coming, but I was somehow not ready.

I believe part of the reason for this is that although you know death will be the final outcome, you still have the individual with you. I could still talk to my husband and discuss current events, the kids, finances, and big decisions that needed to be made. I could still hold his hand, cuddle up to him in the night, tell him I loved him, and hear those words back until he entered the hospital for the final nine days. We were still a couple, united in marriage until death do us part. Nothing can prepare you for this kind of separation. No amount of foreknowledge, medical statistics, prayer, or visualization of the thousands of "death and postdeath" scenarios you come up with. Nothing will prepare you for the tidal wave of death and loss.

Anticipatory grief brings its own difficulties with it. Guilt was one of them for me. Toward the end, I began to want the suffering to end, the same constant stream of words from medical personnel to stop, and the hypervigilance of caring for someone with a serious life-threatening condition to end. I wanted to get on with a normal life and put this behind me. I wanted to do the things I loved once again, like going out to a restaurant, seeing a movie, hiking, going on a holiday, or visiting with friends into the late-night hours free of worry.

I remember longing for the day when I would no longer be listening for my husband's footsteps coming back from the bathroom in the middle of the night or straining to hear his breathing and so many other little things. I desired to be less busy. I was so exhausted and needed rest. We had some struggles financially with all the driving to doctors' appointments, hospital stays, and payments for food and parking. You too may come to the place where you want the pain to stop for your loved one. You will begin to want your life back, and this is normal. These ambivalent feelings of wanting it to end but not wanting them to die are all part of the process of anticipatory grief.

When the moment finally comes, and the death occurs, you may initially feel a great sense of relief; but know this: guilt will follow at some point. Guilt was a relentless battleground for me, playing games in my mind by making me feel more responsible for the outcome than I was. It made me feel like I didn't care enough, should have done more, or wanted it to happen all along. The guilt of anticipatory grief can cause you to get stuck and feel lost in the process of healing if you are unaware that the guilt you feel is false. You are not responsible, and you did everything you could.

I encourage you to find the time and the resources to get good counsel. It is worth it. Your medical team will have access to free in-hospital counseling to help you through the process, but you may need to find a good grief counselor on your own time. Speaking from my own experience, it is money well spent.

Today, when I think back to these comments—"You look like you are handling this very well" and "You knew it was coming"—I can now answer with these words, "No, I was really not doing well, even though I did know it would happen." My world had fallen apart. My husband had died, and I was left standing alone with a hole the size of a bowling ball that went right through my middle. But I looked just fine because of who I am and how I cope. It is important to understand that grief, whether you know it is coming or not, has a force behind it that cannot be comprehended until you are immersed in it.

In this chapter, I have no help or hint on how the caregiver or family should respond to unwanted comments during the celebration of life. I have experienced many losses, and because of that, I feel that the day of the funeral is one day where there ought to be no expectation put upon those who are grieving. The day is hard enough without putting extra pressure on the family to navigate gently around comments and actions that are spoken without thought. The day of the funeral is for everyone who attends, but most importantly, it is for those who have experienced the greatest loss. This day is for them, for the family and closest loved ones. It is a day where closure does not end but rather begins. It is the day that begins the torrent of emotions that will be uncontrollable, as well as unwelcome many times in the days and months that follow.

The day you celebrate the love you lost or a family member you will miss, you should be exempt from having to think through the conversations you will have to find the right words to respond correctly. The day is hard and long; you will do the best you can, and it *will* be enough! Your only goal upon waking should be to make it through the day. And you will. With every fiber of your being, you may not want to do it, but you will anyway—and yes, you can. So take a deep breath, lift your chin up, but put no expectations on yourself that you cannot fulfill.

To those of you who have come to pay your respects to the deceased, your presence is welcome by the family, and it is deeply comforting that you attend. It is good to know that their loved one had touched the lives of each of you in attendance in some way. Or perhaps you are there because you care for a grieving family member. I encourage you not to stay away because you fear saying or doing something wrong. Maybe you have never been to a funeral before, and the thought of attending one makes you uncomfortable. That's OK. Come anyway. I will give you tips on how to best walk this difficult day with your friend. You have already started walking in the right direction by reading this book.

When you speak to the family, give your condolences and let them know you will be thinking and praying for them in the coming months. Do not try to make them feel better by trying to lighten their mood, and please do not try to relate your experience to theirs. Your friends are in pain. Their hearts are broken. Let them know you are sorry for their loss. Let them know that you felt the person who has passed had value to you and that you care about how the family is doing. These things are both welcome and healing. Feel free to let them know why you will miss their loved one if you knew them. Reminisce by telling a story and bring up some positive memories, especially if they will bring a smile to their lips and maybe even some laughter. No memory is too small. I appreciated so much every account of things he had done for and with others. Remember, memories are all they have now, so feel free to add a few to their memory banks.

This day is for grieving and celebrating a well-lived life and a person who will be greatly missed. The Bible says we are to rejoice with those who rejoice and mourn with those who mourn, and the celebration of life is the day to mourn with others. If it looks like they are handling the day well, understand that many dark days are in their future that you will never be aware of. On the other hand, don't let their expressive sorrow make you uncomfortable if they are grieving intensely. Let them handle this day; however they handle it, they are just doing their best to hang on and make it to the end. Support and love are what they need the most, so please be lavish with them.

At the reception, I didn't get a chance to eat because of those who wanted to extend their sympathies. When it was over, I was hungry, exhausted, and emotionally and spiritually depleted. On the day of the funeral, so many emotions, tears, and conversations will tax you that you don't have much energy left by the end. Remember that the family of the deceased has family in town who will likely be converging at their house, and they will not want to cook because they are out of energy. If possible, arrange to have some pizza, or take out of some kind, delivered at around dinnertime, four or five o'clock. This can be costly depending on the size of the family, but coming together with a few friends to help cover the cost is a great way to go if it is too much for you financially. This is a wonderful way to meet an unrecognized need! We had friends who did that for us, which was a welcome and much-appreciated gift! They quietly asked how many I thought would be at my house and told me they would have pizza delivered at five o'clock. I wept at their thoughtfulness.

Remember, you cannot fix their pain or speed up the grief process. It is something they must walk through, and that takes time. In the meantime, from this day forward and in the months and years to come, continue to support, love, and listen whenever you are around them.

Faith and Anticipatory Grief: What Is the Difference?

My faith and relationship with Jesus Christ have always been a place of strength for me and have carried me through many difficult things. Like many of you, I had some childhood traumas to work through, and then I had some of my own decision-making mishaps to take to Him as well. I was familiar with some aspects of grief, as well as other life hardships. I had always been able to find everything I needed when I spent time with Him, even though it was tough. However, I was very unprepared for some things people said to me when James was sick.

The number of times I heard others tell me that "Jesus healed *all*" while James was sick was too numerous to count. Yes, I am aware that He also raised the dead on more than one occasion. It feels repetitive to say, but we did believe in God for healing! We hung on to it like a life rope. But it didn't happen. This may get messy as I maneuver around this topic, so please bear with me and feel free to disagree.

First of all, Jesus never healed *all*, all the time. I understand that this may ruffle a few feathers, but it is true, nevertheless. Let me explain. One day, Jesus went to the Pool of Bethesda, where many sick and injured people were lying around. We have no idea how many were there, but we do know that there was more than one. We understand from reading that one man caught Jesus's eye and heart. Maybe, in his emotional agony and physical disability, he didn't even try to move toward the water anymore. Perhaps he had lost hope and become despondent, and maybe Jesus could see the longing and hope for healing in his eyes.

Whatever it was caught Jesus's attention, and He asked the man if he wanted to get well. The gentleman responded by saying yes, but while the water was being stirred, someone quicker than him could access the pool and receive healing. He realized he needed to be faster to make it into the pool before the others. He knew his limitations. This man was doing all the right things, but he could not access healing on his own. He needed God (John 5:2–9).

Jesus addressed one man lying around the pool, and we are told of only one man who was healed! How did the others feel when Jesus did not heal them? Did they feel condemned because of the events of the day? I wonder if they questioned, "Why him and why not me?" How did they feel as they were left to sit and wait around the pool for their healing?

I am not trying to instill doubt into you, but we must also teach the truth. When we continue to pursue the line of thinking that Jesus healed all, all the time, it leaves us with unanswered questions when our loved one does not get healed. What do we do with our current reality when it doesn't turn out the way we believe it should have? Does healing really boil down to a matter of faith every single time?

I can only speak from my position on this topic, and as each day passed, my ability to "attack" the situation began to falter. It wasn't because I didn't have faith but because I was becoming very, very weary. James, our kids, and I had started strong, loud, and bold. We prayed and worshipped our way through many months. But somewhere around December, about six months after his diagnosis, something shifted. It might have been the brutally honest encounter with Dr. Doom that caused the ground beneath my feet to move, or maybe it was the dream I couldn't forget.

When you add it up with other people's and doctors' words, that dream, and exhaustion, I was left with a measure of guilt when he died. A running cycle of questions haunted me and made me question my faith and my relationship with Jesus. Had I given up? Had I quit? Was I responsible?

The truth is this: my husband did amazingly well! He had been given less than a week, but God pulled him through. He was given a three-month death sentence four times and passed each one with flying colors. He had gone into remission for three months, which we had been told would never happen with the aggressiveness of his cancer. God had indeed answered! We had been granted the privilege of precious time—amazing moments where we bonded, loved, and cherished the time we had left. We had been given a wonderful gift. But then again, we all die, and none of us knows the day or the hour that will happen for us.

Anticipatory grief is a unique gift to you if you allow it to be. It can help soften some of the initial loss you will feel, but it must be allowed to be experienced for that to happen. On the other hand, if we refuse to accept that death could happen, we hinder the process and make the loss that much more difficult.

This can be a real and painful struggle for people of faith, one that I battled so often through the months of sickness. Was he going to be healed? Was he going to die? Were we supposed to continue to pray and believe for complete restoration? Had God given the dream and the months leading up to his death to prepare our kids and me for what would happen? Were we missing the miracle of healing by our lack of faith? Did we have a lack of faith? Many questions ran through my mind and plagued me for a long time.

My advice is to get into the secret place of prayer or silent waiting, ask God what He wants to do, and then move forward in that direction with every fiber of your being. He has a plan, and I don't think we should ever "assume" that we know the will of God, especially if we have not asked or have not been willing to place our agenda and desires before Him.

Please Refrain from Quoting "All Things Work Together for the Good of Those Who Love God and Are Called According to His Purpose" (Romans 8:28)

Romans 8:28 was just one of a stream of scriptures that flowed without any stopping in sight from the woman who stood before me. She had approached me with her husband in tow, tilted her head a little to the right, closed her eyes, and began her recitation. I speak honestly when I say it went on for at least five minutes. Memorized verses meant to heal the brokenhearted but instead felt like an arrow to my heart. When she finally seemed to come to the end of her torrent of words, she opened her eyes, extended her hand, and let me know that she would be praying for me. She then promptly left the building. I remember thinking, *Oh, please, don't!* I am sure she meant to be helpful, but her recitation was cold and impersonal. It was not beneficial to me in any way.

As a Christian and a pastor, I believe strongly in prayer. I also think that as believers, we should know the Word of God thoroughly and take the time to memorize a few verses. However, knowing when to quote, what to quote, and how to quote it is also important to know. (I didn't need to know the citations.) The celebration of life is not the time, and Romans 8:28 is definitely not the verse to quote.

Romans 8:28 seems to be one of the most often-quoted verses during difficulty in people's lives. It sums up in a positive way what cannot be understood while implying that there is something very good on the other side of the pain. I realize this may be true, and good things can follow, but they may not for many months or years afterward. So be kind and don't do it.

Should you quote scripture? Sure! But I think that quoting any verses would be better left until it can be received, and that is when the pain has subsided, and hope is beginning to rise again. The intention was good, but the timing was terrible. Other than this verse, I do not remember any others on her list simply because it was not helping.

What I wanted from her, and what I needed from her, was for her to be personal and real. I was in my most vulnerable moment, and the impression I got from her seemed very distant and uncaring. Funerals and grieving times are a time when the adage "People don't care how much you know until they know how much you care" is very true. The use of this passage, or any others like it, during the moments of the most intense pain dismisses the loss as "part of a better plan." That is like saying God needed to kill your spouse, child, parent, or partner or cause you to lose your job, become homeless, or go through a horrid divorce because He has a better idea in mind.

That is *not* how God works. That is not who He is! He certainly doesn't need to resort to calamity and pain to make good things happen. If He can create an entire galaxy out of nothing, He is certainly not short of ideas or abilities. I advise that scripture of this sort is best left as a tool in the prayer closet when you are crying out to the Lord on behalf of the hurting.

The Word of God should always be welcome for Christians to hear or read. It can bring hope and comfort. It can give direction and stability in difficult times, but perhaps the best place to do this would be in the sympathy card. Just not Romans 8:28. Looking someone in the eye and emotionally letting them know that you are at a loss for words, that you are deeply sorry for their loss, and that you recognize their tremendous loss is much more comforting. Those words bring connection and life because they validate the pain, loss, and heartache. On the day of the funeral, and for many days, weeks, and months after, it is time to mourn with those who mourn.

It is true that God can and will use everything in our lives to bring us closer to Him, including the good, the ugly, and the painful. However, prayer is often the place to work this out with Him. Of course, my boys and I are doing so much better on this side of it, and God has done exactly what this verse promises. But we have also worked through grief issues, cried on one another's shoulders, leaned into the pain, and cried out to God. Time has passed, and that brings healing and closure. I am still young, and I have a deep desire to live life to the fullest. My boys have only begun to taste the fruits of their labors and the pleasures of serving God. We have allowed God to heal the brokenness in our hearts so that we would desire to live fully and enjoy those around us.

One last thing, when you feel like you are at the bottom of life, there is only one direction to go, and that is up, my friend. Remember, you will do better in the future, be better in days to come, and not stay where you are. There is hope! There is always hope!

Remember

For the grieving,

- Give yourself the space to recover emotionally and physically.
- Rest when you can, and try to take the pressure off yourself if you can do so.
- If you need help so you can have some downtime, ask others to help you out.
- Don't be afraid to voice your fears. Death brings up many you are unaware of.
- Beware of the guilt anticipatory grief can leave you in.

For those supporting,

- Do not comment on how a person appears to be handling their grief.
- Let the family know that you are sorry for their loss.
- Do not try to lighten the mood or fix the pain.
- Remember, grief doesn't end when the day is over.
- Provide food for the day of the funeral for the family plus other family members.
- Remember, you cannot fix their pain or quicken their grief process.
- Please don't quote scripture *at* the hurting.
- Scripture quoting is very impersonal.

CHAPTER 8

First and Second Years

When does grieving end? How do you handle your emotions when you are in public? You may have other questions, but these were two of the ones I often found myself struggling with. Finding the answer to them and others like them can be challenging. As difficult as they are, you will inevitably face them as you go.

There are many excellent programs and supports that you can find to ensure that you do not need to remain in a state of constant sorrow indefinitely. I discovered that books where authors told their personal stories were most helpful. I didn't care if the authors were Christian or not because emotions, sorrow, and heartache are universal; therefore, I found each person's story, or parts of their story, relatable. I learned from those who had done this before I had.

YouTube videos and Facebook groups have some great information, discussions, or courses you can sign up for. YouTube is also great for searching selected information. An example of this would be when I was struggling with what to do with our wedding bands or when to let go of the ashes. The videos were also beneficial but very emotional, which was good because they helped me grieve fully. On the other hand, it was the Facebook groups that allowed me to connect with others experiencing loss, and we could reach out to one another without fear of being too vulnerable. It was helpful.

I also went to a grief counselor, where I could tell the story without interruption, suggestions, or discomfort from the one listening to me. This one act was incredibly helpful, but I also did the homework he gave me. With his expertise and wisdom, I realized I was doing fine. He told me I wasn't taking it too hard, wasn't getting stuck, and wasn't too hyperfocused on my pain. He let me know that it was OK to experience my pain, my loss, and my sorrow because that was the best way to recover from it.

In fact, he suggested I put pictures around the house so I would think of him daily. He told me to watch some of James's favorite shows and go to some of his favorite places to help let the emotions out. This led me to begin a yearly weekend away to the mountains for three years, where I would think of him without concern. I found the advice helpful and very therapeutic.

When a friend who had lost her first husband many years prior decided to run a Zoom grief course, I joined; and once again, I found myself growing and healing. All these things helped me lean into my grief and my experience rather than avoid it, and I received more healing. Step by step, I was coming out of the dark and back into a different life than I had known, but one I also knew I wanted to enjoy living.

I encourage you with this: you will find your way through. It won't happen quickly, but please don't think you must do it alone. Look around or have someone else research for you, find the resources you are most comfortable with, and let the resources pull apart the pain so that healing can come.

In your journey, only one person knows how you are doing and how you are feeling, and that person is you! It seemed that I was immediately aware that no one seemed to understand where I was emotionally or why I couldn't make myself bounce back to the happy place I once occupied. You may experience this differently, but while I found the first three months hard, I found months four to six much harder. It was as if this mind-blowing wave of awareness of how badly this sucked and how much I missed James hit me like a train during those months, leaving me reeling many times. But how do you say you feel more broken five months out from the death than you did at first? There is something about grief that is often understated to those who do not go through it and those who are watching you in pain, and that is this: it takes time. It takes time!

Perhaps the reason why months four to six seemed so difficult for me was that the after-death legalities had been completed, and I was left with this niggling feeling that I had just erased James's existence from the earth. But there was another just as sinister part to this process for me: I was realizing that I had lost myself in twenty-eight years of marriage. I had become immersed in my role as a wife and mother, but that had now changed. I was no longer half of what I had been, my children were grown and no longer living in the home, and I was alone!

I was alone! I no longer knew who I was, what I enjoyed doing, or what direction I wanted my life to go. I had no one to discuss this with because the one I would have talked to was no longer there, so I found myself in an identity crisis at fifty-four. I remember panicking the day I realized I had no idea who I was without my husband. I was reading a book on grief by a man who had lost his wife, and I was preparing to do the grief exercise. The homework was that I was to describe who my husband was aside from me and who I was aside from my husband. I couldn't do it.

I found myself at a complete loss. I had no idea who I was. After struggling with the question for at least a week (yes, you read that correctly), I reached out to some friends to help me figure myself out. This exercise was one of the hardest things I needed to do but also one of the most beneficial. At the time, I would have been satisfied to come up with at least three things that described who

I was apart from James; and with the help of friends, eventually, I could do it. It was a beginning.

If you decide to try this, ask yourself these questions: What do you like? What do you want to try? Are you adventurous? Do you like to do physical activity? Gardening? Do you find satisfaction in helping other people? Would you like to get involved in volunteering? Take the time to explore who you are, and then enjoy the you, you find. Don't rush yourself, though; this is not an easy thing to do. If you do the exercise, I don't think you will regret it!

Time was passing, but I was still very affected by sleepless nights, which were getting old, and I was still feeling unwell in so many ways. This wasn't my first loss, having lost both of my parents many years before, yet I had no idea that grief could affect every single aspect of my life the way it did. Thankfully, my family physician is very thorough and wanted to ensure I was fine. I had multiple appointments, ultrasounds, blood work, and more. The reality was I did not feel well, but the evidence proved otherwise. Grief is hard.

The first year is more than birthdays, holidays, and anniversaries. It includes the first load of laundry that holds only your clothes and grocery shopping that looks significantly smaller and without your person's preferred items like cheese was for me. It includes first oil changes, first flights alone, first time eating alone at home or in a restaurant, one dish, a single fork, and a single glass in the sink. It can include celebrating weddings and engagements and inviting the first grandchild into the world by yourself, knowing they would have wanted to be there. Your events may differ significantly, but they will all leave their mark on your heart. They will be hard and lonely, and they will all suck.

For these unspoken reasons and many others, we should not look at the grieving and tell them that they should be further along than they are or that they should not grieve as if they had no hope (another unhelpful Bible verse sent my way from 1 Thessalonians 4:13). I had hope knowing I would see him again, but I was grieving. I guess you could say I was grieving with hope in mind. What you need to know is that I missed his company here. I know where he is, but I missed him here. His parents missed him here. His sister missed him here. Our children missed him here.

I have realized it is OK to grieve deeply without apologizing as long as you don't stay there. I understood that my children, church, extended family, and others who have yet to cross my path need me and will continue to need me. Your people will need you too. Regardless of what you are going through, keep going. You are needed. You are loved. Please don't give up. Don't quit even when it feels like you have nothing left to live for.

One of the greatest blessings for me during this time was to be included in the gatherings of friends. What a wonderful feeling it was to be invited to lunch after church or dinner at a restaurant. A fun day out doing something—anything—was life-giving and welcome. The problem was it didn't happen very often. By this time in my walk, I understood that grief and mourning make people uncomfortable, and I also realized that I would probably not be the life of the party. It just seemed like very few people were willing to take the chance to invite me out, so I spent a considerable time alone. Unfortunately, as I have talked to others who have gone through troubling shifts in life, like divorce, death, career loss, illness, or mental health issues, it seems this is all too common.

I admit that being invited out can feel like a gamble, even to yourself, when you realize that each day is emotionally very different from the one before and after. Accept that you are on this roller coaster, and instead of making long-term plans for big events, wait to see how you are on the day of and then decide. One of the reasons this can be so difficult is that you may feel like you have lost your security. You may no longer know who you are or how or what you will have to contribute to a group setting. Only you know how vulnerable you feel. When the outing comes up, if you can't do it, you can't do it! Could you repeat after me, "It is OK to back out"?

For those of you considering sending the invitation to include the vulnerable, do it! Remember, if you extend the invitation to have tea, go out for dinner, go shopping, or go to a movie, please ensure you carry through with these plans. Otherwise, these invitations become words without substance and are deeply felt by the grieving as another loss. The feeling of no longer fitting in is marked even more, which can make someone in a delicate situation feel obligated to go to an event or home even if they don't feel like they can do it on the day.

I wanted so badly to be a part of a life-giving event. Sometimes, this turned out very well, and I could enjoy myself. At other times, I wanted to hide in a corner and go home sooner rather than later. It took me some time to be kind to myself as I grappled with the fact that my world was having a massive shift. I made it through, and you will make it as well. Just breathe!

Following through with your invitations to those in turmoil is vitally important during times like this, even if it makes you a little nervous, considering the possible outcomes. The person you are considering inviting or not inviting is not looking for attention or pity. They just have no idea how to fit in in their new normal, and they need time and experience to build a new foundation in this area. They still want to have fun and be around other people but don't know how they will handle the crowds, questions, and conversations. Your only responsibility is to invite them and let them feel however they are going to feel. It may go well, and it may not. If they become overwhelmed, cry, and need to go home, release them, love them, support them, and check in with them soon after. Then, please do it again! Please don't let too much time pass before you extend the invitation once more, keeping in mind that the turnaround point will come. In the meantime, they need to know they are loved and accepted.

I found a recurring theme in the critical moments of James's health journey. There were always many people around initially when he had his heart attack, when he was diagnosed with leukemia, and after he passed. The phone calls came often, inquiring about his health. Text messages came almost daily, while visitations were less frequent. However, as time ticked by, we found that these things were happening much less until they had dried up almost completely within a few short weeks.

If you decide that you are going to be a support person for someone who is mourning or struggling, please don't put a time limit on your care, love, or support. I had someone I had always considered a good friend tell me that they would be there for me initially, but I should not get too excited because it wouldn't last forever. At least, she was honest and true to her word. In less than three months, she told me she had spent her time, and it was up to me to work it out. She rarely checked in with me after that. Please don't do this. Understand that being there initially only to remove your support when you feel you are done only creates more pain and isolation for the one not finished grieving. Grief is a process. It takes time, and I encourage you to be there through the entire journey if possible.

A Word To Those Who Are Caregivers and Wounded

To those of you who are suffering, I want you to know you will make it through your trial. At one point, I looked like I had lost many friends; and unfortunately, it turned out to be true for some of them but not all. Some forever changed the kind of relationship we had as they distanced themselves from me for a time. My part in the ebb and flow of these relationships was to forgive and decide how to move forward when and if they returned. You may find this to be your struggle as well. On the bright side, I have found many new friends who understand my heart and pain and are willing to support me whenever needed. I found that some of those relationships I considered gold before only became more polished through the years, and these friends continually walk alongside me.

It is the friends who loved me enough not to leave me when I was difficult, angry, raging, and lashing out as I tried to deal with my grief. (You know who you are.) Thank you. Then, some emerged from nowhere, holding me up, listening to me, and speaking words of encouragement and life into me when I needed it most. The reality is you may experience all this and more.

True, refined, God-given friendships are forged in the fire; and once you have made it through and are standing on the other side of your valley, there isn't much that will be able to separate these relationships. You may look at where you are in a few years and realize that you have an almost-new circle of friends, with the old faded and gone in the haze of history. Rejoice in the ones you have around you. Rejoice in the ones who came through with you. Rejoice in the ones left standing. They are a precious gift!

Year Two and Fighting Giants

Many books on the first year of grief and loss cover the emotional turmoil that seemingly erupts out of nowhere. These books cover some great insights and are extremely helpful when and if you need them. Take advantage of those who have paved the way before you. But the reality is that as difficult as the first year was, no one seems to talk about year two! The second year was a giant in its own right.

It struck me hard when I realized with finality that this was not the first Christmas, birthday, or anniversary but the second. The haunting reality of this seemed to continue to chime like a huge bell ringing out the hour of the day in my heart. "It was really over!" I was struck with the fact, hit with the cold harshness, that he was never, ever coming back. It was over, and I was alone and would have to do this day again and again. I would face another year without him. I dreaded that prospect, and I seemed very unprepared for it, to be honest.

Perhaps the reason I felt so ill prepared was because I had done my grief work. I had taken the classes, read the books, seen a grief counselor, and leaned into the experience. I realized that all the information I had absorbed and all the work I had done was for the first year alone. What a surprise that year two could be so much easier in some ways and yet uniquely much harder in others.

The decisions that needed to be made now did not include what food to serve at the funeral, when to go to the bank to close accounts, how to send documents to proper people, or how to remove his name from many accounts—those things had been settled. The issues that held my attention were much more personal. The things that were tripping points in the first year no longer bothered me, and I knew that I had grown and had become more confident in my abilities. I had done the "firsts." I had cried, healed, and grown.

However, that other side of the bed seemed like it was still off-limits, almost like it was sacred ground. It felt odd to consider sleeping on the side of the bed he had occupied for nearly twenty-eight years. Logically, I could process that it was just a bed, and I could sleep anywhere I wanted to in it. But I could not. As I began to tackle this giant, I set a goal and began to pray. Very slowly, I began inching myself over to "his" side of the bed. I sleep there regularly now, but it was a giant to conquer, and it took time. My hollowness was repaired and never returned once I made the adjustment.

The wedding ring I wore became a constant reminder of what I no longer had. But the question was, when do I remove it? Do I remove it? Somehow, it felt dishonoring to my vows, to our love, and to my husband to remove it, even though those vows did say till *death* do us part. I began watching YouTube videos of other widows who struggled with the same decision and sobbed. I took some of the advice I heard and started the process. My first step was to remove my ring and place it, along with James's wedding band, on a gold chain, which I wore around my neck for several months.

It felt strange; at first, my heart hurt, my gut felt empty, and my finger felt uncomfortably bare. Daily, I continued to wear the rings around my neck until it no longer bothered me. Then, I placed the chain with the rings on a jewelry hook so that I could visibly see them every day. I continued to wear the chain when I felt vulnerable, alone, or lonely. Finally, I put them in my jewelry box, where they stayed. Giants!

Another question to be tackled in year two was what to do with the house. Do I sell and move, or should I stay? Where would I go? What does starting over look like for me? I live in a four-level split, and this is way too much house for a single woman and her cat. I began the process of painting as I mulled over my options and talked to a real estate agent.

It became clear that I needed the first year to decide if I could do all the work associated with living in a house alone. In the second year, I needed to determine if I wanted to do all the work independently. Questions I could not answer in the first year could be and would be answered in the second. Two of the biggest were whether I would find the work overwhelming or satisfying. As the second year rolled through, I decided to stay. The decision was made easier with the assistance of my oldest son and his wife, who live nearby and are a godsend for me when I need them most and even when I don't. They help me with many things, even when I don't ask. They do it all willingly, with love and appreciation for both me and his dad.

My struggle with what to do with the house was not clouded by memories because I held them in my heart. The house is not a chamber of remembrance for me. This house is where I live and where my children come to visit. This is a giant that many of you will contend with, and it cannot be taken lightly. We all store our memories in different ways. For some, it is the tangible things that bring experiences and memories alive for them, while for others, it is not. I empathize with those who struggle because it is not easy. It is a big decision.

I waited until year two to even consider putting the first item of his clothing into a bag and taking the time to consider the tools in the garage, his motorbike, as well as other personal items. Each thing I did took time. I didn't want to erase him from my life too quickly or thoroughly because I never knew when I might need something of his, and I needed time to process and grieve. Downsizing is never fun, especially when it is forced upon you. Giants!

The examples I've shared are what second-year hurdles can look like, but there are many more, and there will be some unique to your situation and relationship. Grief is not the only thing that brings these giants. Divorce holds many of the same ones. Perhaps you don't need to decide what to do with property, but you may be struggling financially like never before. Maybe you can no longer appreciate your love of travel because of financial stress, fear of traveling alone, or stress-related illness. All these losses must be grieved as well so that you can move forward into a completely joy-filled life once again.

These were some of the things I was mulling over that few people could understand or relate to. I was fighting giants that very few people knew about, so being told that I had a *spirit of heaviness* on me since my husband's death was not helpful or something I needed to hear. I was at a loss for words. There seemed to be no way I could articulate what I had already overcome or what I was currently overcoming without it sounding like an excuse for my emotional state. I was sad. That should have been expected. I had compiled grief with other family losing their fight to cancer also. I was not stuck—I was fighting! I was grieving. I was broken.

I was in the process of walking *through* the healing, and I was feeling the waves of sorrow as each person passed from this life. I was fighting giants that only a few individuals knew anything about, and sometimes, even those who knew did not really get it. Grief is hard. Don't feel the need to make excuses for it, be something you are not, or feel something you are incapable of feeling or doing. You are doing fine, and you will come through!

Today, I can articulate what I could not at that time; there were times I was sad because of how his death had affected those around me and others who were close to him. The tough stuff we go through is never just about us, but this was again something I could not say without bringing offense to those I spoke it to. The conversations I would have with my in-laws, my sister-in-law, my children, or his best friend were heartbreaking. His loss was not just mine! Talking to these individuals as they processed their grief also affected me.

I began to know my husband in ways I had not known him, and that was through the eyes and hearts of others. I started to learn things about him and the way he interacted with others. He loved many people and helped them find and become their best selves. It was heartwarming but bittersweet to get a glimpse of the man I did not know. I began to understand that my loss was the loss of many; it's just that mine was very different. I saw how well he loved others through the love and loss others experienced for him. These are giants that need to be overcome!

I quickly realized that as deep and painful as my grief was, it paled in comparison to his parents' grief. There is something about a parent losing a child that goes beyond the marriage bond. For a mother who carries a child in her womb, nurses them, raises them, loves them, protects them, and releases them, that loss is inexplicably painful. I could do nothing but weep with my parents-in-law as I listened and loved him even more for who he was to them while my heart was shattered for them. Yes, my loss was the loss of many.

Please Don't Ask about Cremation and the Spreading of the Ashes

After pondering his options, James decided that he wanted to be cremated. It was his decision. Although I tried to find out his reasoning, he was never forthcoming with the information, so I needed to settle into accepting it. I was not too fond of the decision initially, but in the end, it didn't seem like something to argue about. There were always more important issues at hand that required my attention and energy.

I found it interesting, and still do, how people reacted to the knowledge of how James decided to handle his body after death. It generated a lot of conversations and many opinions, most of which came once again from what they would do if it were them. The thing is, it wasn't them—it was James. This is what he had chosen, and I decided to honor his decision. As I have mentioned earlier, the concept of cremation seems to be a hurdle many Christians cannot reconcile or accept.

I am sure that had he chosen to be buried, very few, if any, questions would have been asked. For some reason, cremation makes many people uncomfortable. I handled this by repeatedly answering the questions and saying I wasn't sure of all his reasons, but it was his choice. As his wife, I wanted to honor him. That caused most of the conversations to come to an end.

In hindsight, I think part of the problem was that his ashes would be in my house. Somehow, people thought that couldn't be emotionally or mentally healthy for me or the boys. People were concerned for me, and I appreciate that today; but to put things in perspective, it is a personal decision, not one that others can dictate. I have since talked to some widows whose spouses had been buried, and they would spend significant time at the graveside for many months. The visits would include everything from bad days to first birthdays, anniversaries, or holidays. They would go to the place where their husband's body lay, and no one questioned it or commented on it. Yet somehow, having the ashes of your loved one in your house seemed morbid, odd, and unacceptable.

I was repeatedly told that it would be a good idea to get rid of the ashes as soon as I could and asked whether I didn't find it uncomfortable that I was keeping them in the living room. Where was I supposed to keep them? In the closet? Or behind other closed doors so that others were not uncomfortable? I still have this question: why is it more acceptable to picnic at the graveyard than having your loved one in a cabinet?

In either situation, graveyard or cabinet, the body's remains are the same. They are remains—a body. The man I loved is no longer here on the earth, and the person you love is no longer on the planet. Whether you visit them in a graveyard or have them in your cupboard, you are grieving the soul of a loved one. Don't allow others to tell you an acceptable way for you to do so. We, as a family, are all far enough along in our grief journey to let him go.

Spreading the ashes was not a decision that I could make alone. It included his parents, my children, and his sister. When was everyone ready to release him? Once again, I have been faced with the truth that the decision is not only mine to make. It belongs to us all, and I want desperately to include his mother in the timing of it. When that day comes, we will unite one more time as a family and celebrate a man we loved deeply. We will laugh, but we will probably also cry. We will tell stories and eat cheese. We will honor him one last time, and we will walk away better people for having known him.

Remember

For those dealing with grief,

- Find resources you feel comfortable with and begin to work through your loss and pain.
- It isn't just the first birthday, anniversary, and holiday that are hard. It is the everyday things as well.
- Grief is about missing your person and has nothing to do with where their remains rest.

For Those Supporting

- Do not avoid those who are grieving.
- Invite them to parties, gatherings, and events. Then, let them decide to come or stay home.
- If you must postpone your gathering, make sure you follow through at a later date.
- Even if they crack under pressure, make sure you invite them out again.
- The hurting is not looking for pity. They are temporarily broken.
- Don't make the struggling feel like they are stuck in the grief they feel.

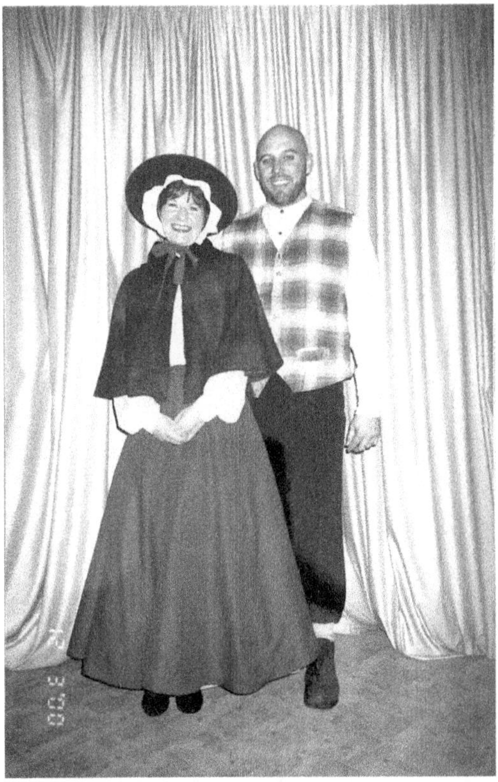

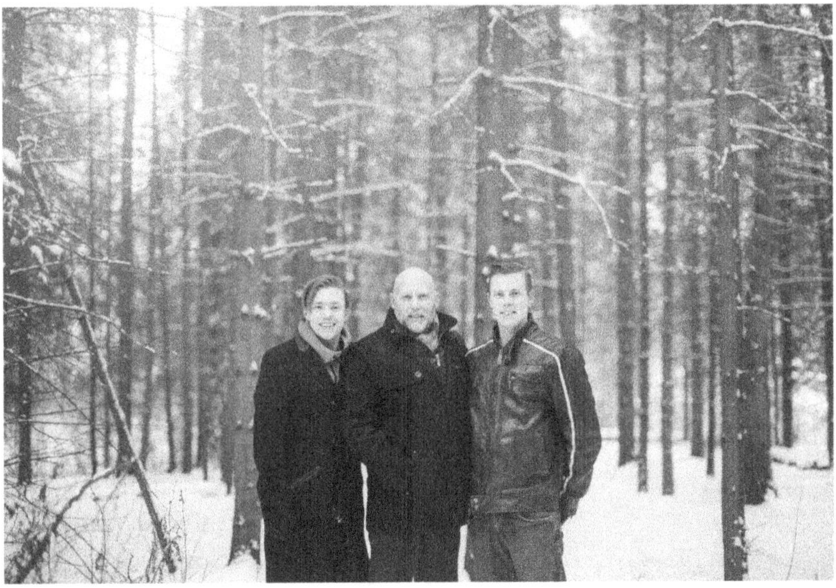

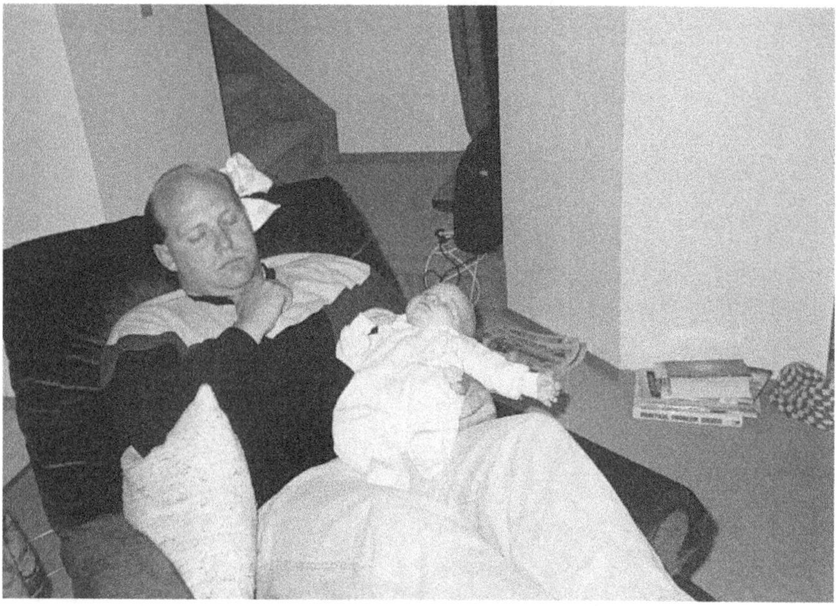

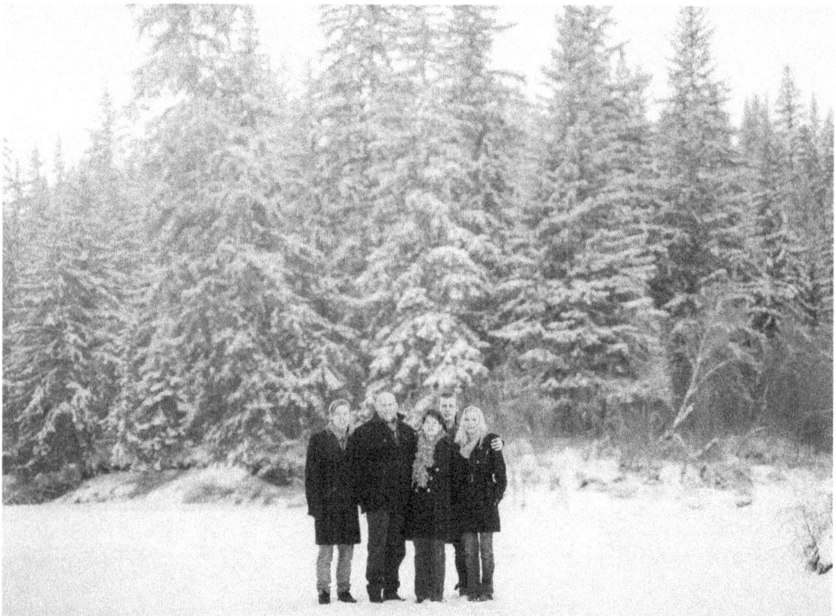

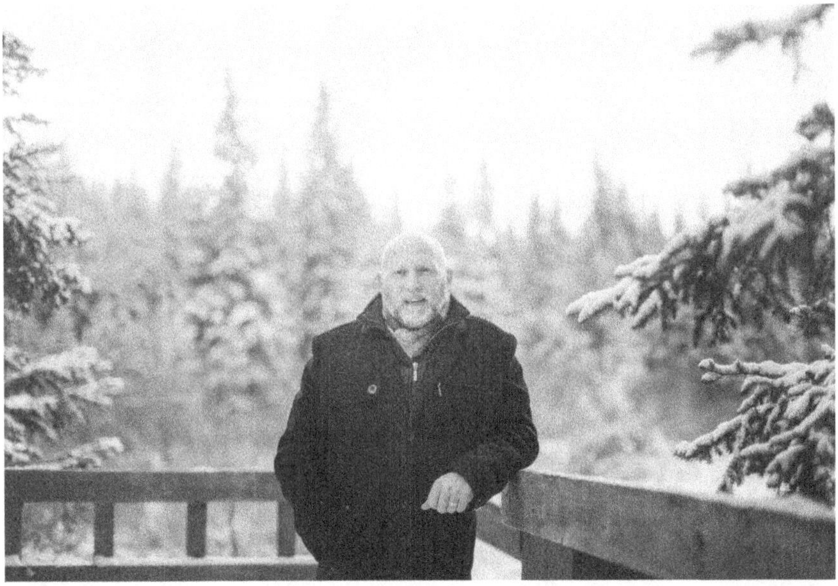

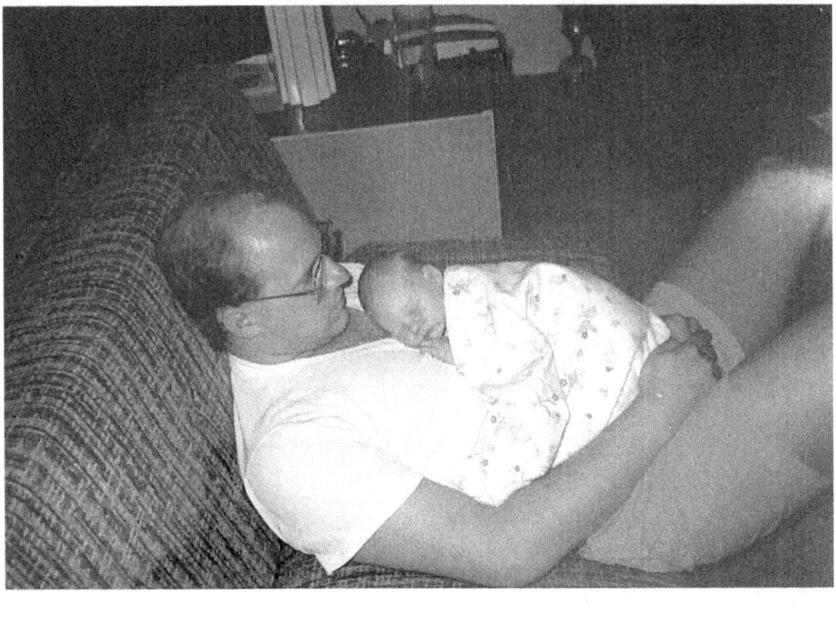

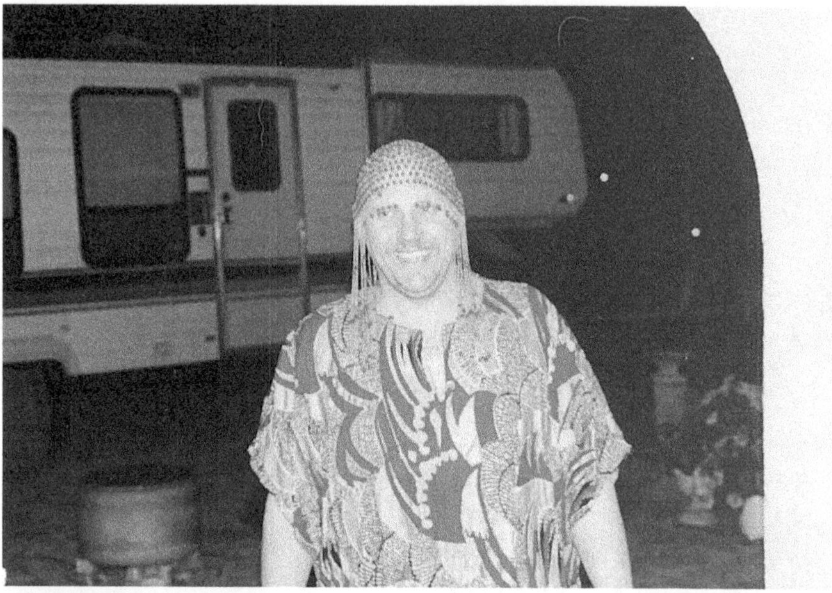

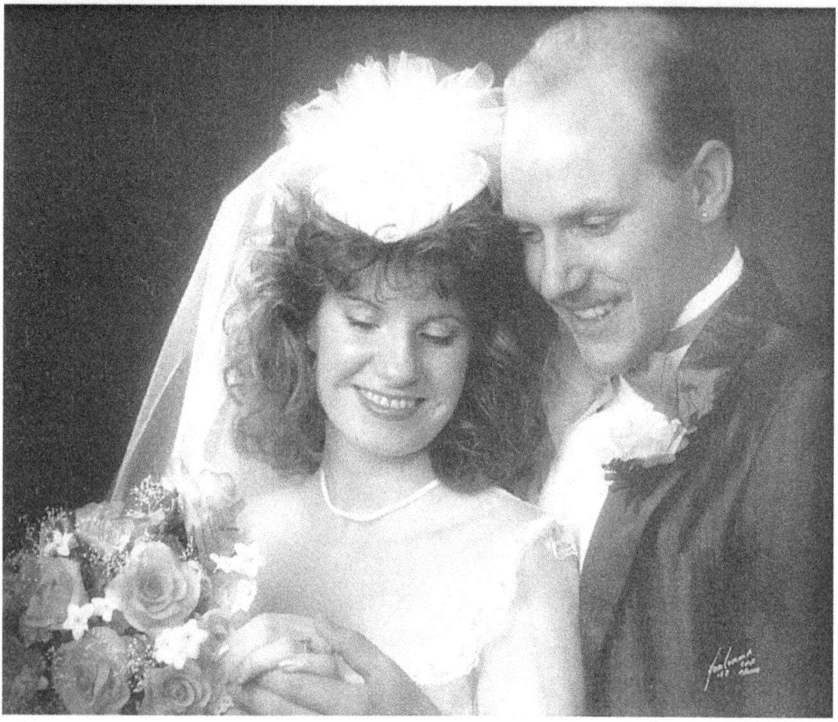

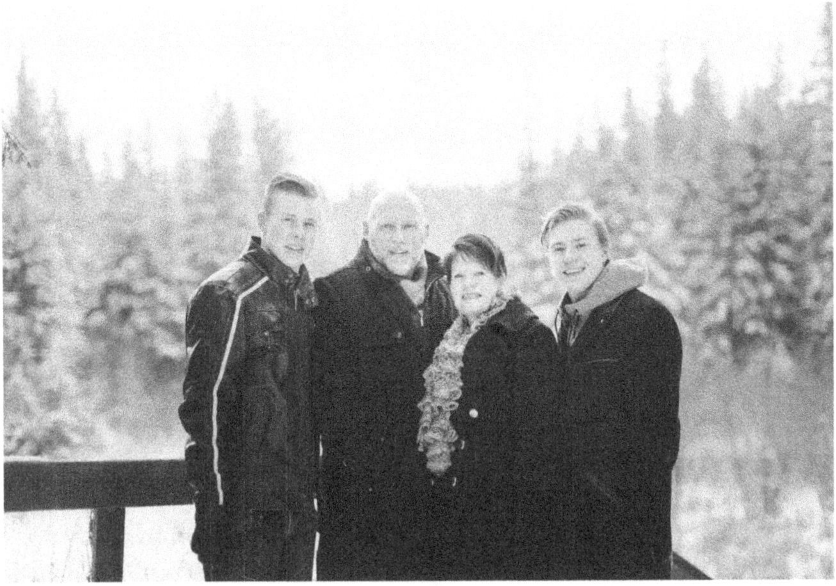

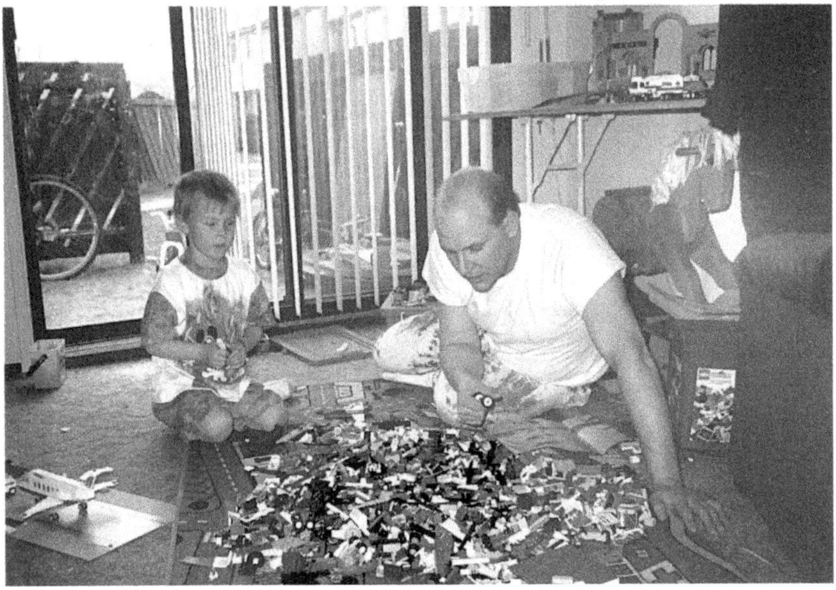

Family pictures

CHAPTER 9

Taking Personal Responsibility

Making Your Way through the Anger

It was amazing to discover that grief expresses itself in so many emotions. It didn't take long before I realized that grief expresses itself in fear, but as time passed, I realized that it also expresses itself through anger. You may have already known both of these things. Although I had heard that anger is a part of grief, it was a very different thing to experience it than to know about it.

I had a prior understanding that fear is part of grief, so I tried to accept it as such, knowing that it was OK to be feeling fear and that it would pass. I felt the anger in much the same way, yet I didn't understand where that underlying anger came from. Fear and anger were both just there! I didn't know what to do with either of them and had no idea how to get rid of them, as they would rear their heads at the oddest of times.

As I worked my way through the process, I found myself struggling with some basic control issues. I often felt so completely out of control. I couldn't control the deaths that kept coming. I couldn't manage my health, which seemed unpredictable, as I kept having things pop up without warning. My mind was acting like a chaotic, swirling mess of thoughts, like a sieve in which I could not retain the simplest of thoughts or tasks. I was out of control emotionally, or so it felt. No matter how many times I mentioned certain things to people around me, it went unheeded. Some of my friendships were falling apart, and my ability to read the Bible and pray seemed to have also abandoned me. At some point, I remember telling someone that I felt like I was in an eddy that was sucking me downward while I was desperately swimming with everything I had, trying to survive!

I wasn't sure if the above was exactly how it was supposed to be, but it was, and perhaps that is part of where the anger came from. Anger is part of the grief process. This truth has been written about in many books and discussed by therapists throughout the years. I cannot, however, ever remember a single explanation for this anger beyond that some have anger toward the person who died while others are angry with God. Yet neither of these was true for me.

I wasn't angry with my husband for dying because I knew he didn't want to die and did everything he could to live. This doesn't mean I was never angry because he wasn't around. There were times when I needed help with something or couldn't figure something out, and these things brought me to tears as the anger pushed upward and outward, but I was not angry with him for dying. I was also not angry with God for not healing him and allowing him to die. I understood that He had been preparing me for James's departure far longer than I was willing to admit.

I wanted to know why! Here's a little background so you will understand why I have the question. I will start with the fact that the Lord audibly told me to marry James three times while we were dating. I wanted God to answer the question, "Why would you tell me to marry him and then take him home so early in his life?" That seemed like a reasonable question. My interpretation of that statement from God was that, surely, we would live a full life together. We would grow old together. Additionally, because of our family health history, I fully expected to be the first to go. Yet none of that is what happened. I realize now that these were my expectations. I was angry because they had not been met, and I did not have a reasonable answer for why they were not.

However, other reasons associated with death can cause anger to surface. If we leave any lack of forgiveness toward the dead or others who have said or done things, we will become angry; and if we have unresolved anger, we can eventually become bitter. I found myself angry at the mostly unspoken yet subtly suggested ways that I, the person handling the trauma and loss, was expected to be responding. The message I heard was that I was not meeting expectations. When I mentioned this to someone I hoped would help, I was admonished not to say anything because it would hurt the other person's feelings. Comments like these only added to the burden of grieving.

I understand that the words spoken to me were likely said with good intentions; however, they were not coming from a place of experience, and that is what made them even more wounding. Being told I couldn't say anything protected them, allowing them to continue speaking and doing hurtful things. We must be able to voice our experiences in our most vulnerable times and be accepted when we do it. We should not be silenced and, therefore, allow the hurt to continue to come our way. It wasn't the right thing to say, but I finally told the person who counseled me this way that it was like telling an abuse survivor not to tell her abuser that they hurt her because it would hurt his feelings.

This needs to stop! If we are to be a community that walks with the hurting, this really does need to stop! Abuse, misunderstanding, isolation, depression, and ultimately more wounding will continue if we do not address the need to support those in pain. As we continue to tolerate and accept the hurtful things said by defending callous and damaging statements, we will not—and we cannot—bring the wounded to a place of wholeness. Hurting people must be heard and allowed to have a voice that expresses without guilt or condemnation exactly how they are doing.

The things we go through in life do shape us, like it or not. For example, I have a cat, Lucky, who survived a house fire. The trauma of that experience is noticeable anytime the wind is high or there is a thunderstorm. He is inconsolable and often hides behind the washer and dryer until well after the storm has ended. When people are over, they see his panic and anxiety and have compassion for him. That fire was over nine years ago. Should we not expect him to have gotten over it? If the answer is no, then why is it that we expect that the first three months are all that is needed to properly grieve a massive life shift like death, divorce, or illness?

It takes time to recover from painful life events. Emotional healing from difficulty and hardship takes more than a three-month adjustment period. In some cases, it is lifelong. The first year or two holds a lot of uncertainty as those going through it struggle to redefine, accept, and live in their new normal. It takes time to get your feet under you again and begin to feel comfortable, so keep in mind that the words you say are felt deeply whether they are meant to wound or not.

While all this is true, there is something we need to keep in mind: we are responsible for what we say and how we react, and that goes for every person involved in the journey. I said very little most of the time when I was approached by a strange and hurtful comment that left me undone, which meant that I needed to do much processing of the things that had been said while I was alone. We have no control over what others say or do, but we can watch our words and actions. I write these words in an effort to ease the pain and further suffering of others. If that is the result, then every word written and every experience I had will be worth it.

In any massive life shift, regardless of what it is, there is a dynamic loss of stability. The things we have taken for granted in our previous, unscarred lives can often no longer be leaned upon. When life as we know it becomes fractured or permanently damaged, we are forced to find a new way of thinking and determine where our faith really lies.

When I was growing up, I knew a man who had lost his arm in a farm accident. In every way imaginable, he was as normal as possible; yet when he would visit the restaurant I was employed in, he needed me to cut his meat. It might seem like a little thing, but he could not do it. What would have happened if I had refused? He would not be able to enjoy his meal, he would look foolish, and he would most definitely become frustrated with my lack of support.

In the long run, the biggest changes to be made had to come from him. He needed to relearn many, many things. While we take for granted tasks like writing, putting on socks and pants, or buttoning a shirt, he needed to relearn them all, plus much more. Regardless of the many things he found himself able to accomplish, cutting his steak in a restaurant was something he would never be able to do on his own. He needed the help of other people. There is another side to this coin, and that is that he also needed to admit that he needed help.

We are responsible for who we are and how we handle what we go through, but we are equally responsible for handling the fragility of those in need. This man would seldom eat out without the ability to voice his needs. But it is equally important to note that if no one was willing to accommodate him, he would also be unwilling to subject himself to the humiliation of dining out.

I use this illustration to show that the biggest change was happening in the man who lost his arm. He had the most adjustments to make, the most to relearn, the most inner trauma to deal with, and the most healing to overcome. As much as this is true, he would always need others to help him with some of the tasks we take for granted. Grief, loss, and other dramatic life changes run parallel to this story. Simply put, sometimes we need others to cut our meat for us.

Please Don't Say, "You Will Figure It out"

"If you need anything, just ask"—a six-word sentence that was repeated more times than I could count. I believed the words to be true, and I thought that those who said them meant what they spoke, and yet it took me so long to get the courage to ask for help. I might have felt that asking for help was admitting I was incapable, a failure, or weak. The truth is it was just pride, and it wasn't an admission to anything other than the fact that I needed some assistance.

I pulled every ounce of courage I had together and asked for help, but the response I got was "You will figure it out. Other people have, and you will too." The person in front of me quickly crossed the street, got into their vehicle, and drove away, leaving me standing in the driveway of another individual we had met with. The thing I found hardest to work through was that this man had offered his assistance, extending these six words repeatedly, and I thought he was sincere. I am trying to remember how I responded. I believe I just got into my vehicle, slammed the door, and drove off with the comment ringing in my ears. It had taken me so long to accept that others might be willing to help if asked, yet his statement slammed the door tightly on any further requests I might have. I admit that my attitude was not right, but the words felt like they sliced right through me.

Anger at thoughtless and unkind words that were unintentionally wounding was a constant battle in the first two years. Behind the words "You will figure it out" was the unspoken yet equally powerful statement, "You are inconveniencing me"—or at least that is what I heard and believed. I quickly realized that second-year problems came surging in with second-year rage! What I had not said, but should have, was that I had learned how to do many things on my own and would not be asking for help if I did not need it. In time, I would tell this friend exactly that and let him know how deeply his words affected me.

This encounter had a positive side because the comment propelled me to pull up my bootstraps and get help from those who were willing, even if I needed to pay for it, which I did most of the time. I found freedom in doing it this way. The ability to pay gave me privileges I would not have known otherwise. If I was unsatisfied with the job done, I could say so; and even though this was difficult for me initially, it became easier as I went. Hiring someone to do a job for you puts you in a position to speak out kindly about changes you want done. I began to feel like a client, not a burden. Hiring help may not be an option for many of you because of finances, and for many more, you may never face this situation. What I do hope is that you never hear those words when you reach out.

The truth is there will be many things you will figure out in the first two years. One of the biggest challenges will be to *walk in forgiveness*. You cannot fully eliminate your anger toward others if you are unwilling to forgive them. If you are stuck on the hamster wheel of reliving conversations, unable to forgive and let go of the pain, you will find yourself avoiding these people so that you do not feel the wound again. Avoidance is not forgiveness. Avoiding those who have hurt you will give you a false sense of peace and, many times, even a false sense of joy. When left untouched and unhealed, anger and unforgiveness will open the door to bitterness, and no one wants to go there. It is a vicious cycle that seems to have no end.

Forgiving others who have hurt you can be a big undertaking, but living with unforgiveness and anger can and will affect your health. Unforgiveness can also make us cynical and critical of everything and everyone, most especially those who have wounded us. Refusing to forgive will only further your isolation and pain and keep you stuck indefinitely. When you forgive a person for a wrong committed, it does not mean that you are saying they did nothing wrong, did not hurt you, or that what they did was OK. What forgiveness does is allow you to heal from the wound and move on with your life.

Forgiveness should include accepting and acknowledging that you have been unjustly treated, but it also allows you to realize you don't need to carry the load of it forever. It is one of the most important hurdles to overcome to recover from traumas or life-altering events. Remember, you are not letting them off the hook for what they said or did, but you are letting yourself off the pain-train loop. Forgiving them allows you to come to them afterward and tell them civilly and with dignity, without the punchiness of anger behind your words, that what they said or did hurt you and why. But even if you never tell them, you are still released from the effects of it.

I needed to take this approach with my friend, and I knew it. I also knew that I had to deal with the pain those words caused me, or my delivery would cause further distress to us both, possibly ending our relationship. The truth is, I found the relationship we had valuable, so I was more interested in salvaging it than ending it. We sat in a coffee shop, and I told him how that comment felt like a kick in the gut to me when he had said it. I also let him know that I thought he had let me down in this area. He had consistently said, "Anything you need, just ask," but I struggled because he hadn't meant what he had said.

Initiating this conversation gave me the opportunity for an open dialogue, explanations to be given, and a heart-to-heart discussion that brought us closer in the long run. I had never considered how difficult the loss of my husband had been on him. It was hard for him to see me in pain, and he felt woefully ill-equipped to deal with it. He explained that on the day I asked for help, he was unprepared to handle what I had asked. He said he had several other things to do but admitted the mishandling of my request. He apologized. I forgave him face-to-face this time after wrestling with it privately. I also asked for his forgiveness as I confessed my feelings toward him and the rage that had surfaced. He was gracious to forgive me.

This was not how I would handle every situation, of course, but it was how I chose to deal with many of the relationships I valued. God was deepening my understanding of forgiveness and confrontation for a godly purpose that brings restoration. I was relearning the Matthew principle: "If you have something against your brother, go to him."

I applied it with mostly good results. *Confrontation* is not a dirty word if done after your heart has had the opportunity to be reconciled in forgiveness and recognition of your own relational shortcomings.

As painful as it is to admit, although many things will happen to each of us and cause us pain, we, the grieving and hurting, must take responsibility for ourselves and our actions. We cannot continually blame others for our responses; finger-pointing is never the answer.

Doing that will not bring freedom but rather further isolation. I needed to do my part so that I could reason through and accept that people around me had things they too were struggling with.

While in Pain, Be Careful Not to Drink from the Wrong Stream

Again, I want to mention how imperative it is to find your support people as early as possible because this is a key to your healing. What I share now is an example of what can happen when you find yourself too tightly connected with the wrong comforters.

In my loneliness and brokenness, I was willing to allow myself to be hosted by almost anyone willing to invite me into their world. It was an experience that was unusual for me and not something I had struggled with prior. My emotional upheaval resulted in some wrong choices of friendships because my discernment seemed to have taken a hiatus. It put me in a few vulnerable situations, one of which I regretted in the long run. I will take full responsibility for this myself because no one else is to blame. I was vulnerable and broken, but I was also angry. In the above example, the person I lashed out at was a good friend, and I had been hurt by an insensitive response. When someone came along and agreed with my pain by questioning his integrity and care for me, I listened. Listening was my first mistake. My second was in responding in agreement to what had been said.

It can be way too easy to get entangled in conversations we should not have when everything is going well, but it can be much easier when we are in pain and feel misunderstood. I admit that I still don't fully know the hearts of those who fed me the wrong messages, but I do know that I drank too deeply of the things they said. I not only listened at times but also allowed myself to meditate on them, and that made me feel worse overall. I don't want to spend too much time on this one area, but I do want to bring it to light because it is what I often see being played out in those going through "stuff."

Please pay attention to the conversations you are having. If they begin to bring suspicion against another person's character, you need to remove yourself regardless of how badly you feel you need the contact. I admit it can feel good to have your hurt feelings soothed, but remember, gossip is a form of passive-aggressive anger. It may make you feel good for a while, it may make you feel validated for a time, but it is misplaced, and it will end up hurting not just you but everyone involved. Talking behind closed doors will not solve your problems, but it can and likely will create more, so try to end these types of conversations as quickly as you can.

The conversations to avoid include dropping little innuendos regarding why something was said or done. These little droplets from others may be unintentional, but if they cause you to think less of a person than you did before, it is up to you to correct it and not think about it. The hypersensitivity you feel when in pain won't last forever, but it can make you feel like what you hear confirms what you suspect about someone who has recently spoken an insensitive comment to you. I assure you, it is likely not true. When we are in an emotional place like grief, where we tend to hide many intense emotions, the last thing we should be doing is making a judgment call on someone else's character, especially if they have been one who has said something they shouldn't have said.

Conversations that feed our pain are different from those that draw it out. The first is like dropping acid onto a solid surface and slowly watching it erode, while the other may bring tears but aid us in the healing process. The acid may feel refreshing at first, but ultimately, it will destroy you and those relationships in question, even if, at the moment, it can feel like a cooling, fresh drink of water. Remember, healing takes time, but lashing out in conversation or listening to ones that blur the reputations and characters of people not included in the discussions are ones you may regret in the long run. It is always best to only engage once you can respond with a healed heart.

Avoid conversations where others agree with your feelings of being unappreciated, unwanted, like you are "doing it wrong," or

WHAT NOT TO SAY

conversely, those that make you feel like you are better or are doing better than you really are. Challenging life circumstances put most of our attention on ourselves and how we think and feel, to begin with. Hearing that we are unappreciated will feed and grow further rejection until it consumes us, especially if we have already been feeling an intense lack of appreciation or value. (This can often come with all types of loss.) Our perceptions during grief can be skewed. Once more, I encourage you to avoid, when possible, the conversations that make you feel more isolated or angrier when you leave.

Anger can be a genuine and powerful emotion to deal with. Unlike fear, which will mostly merely isolate you, anger can be very destructive. Anger is easy to justify, especially when we have proof that the offense is valid, and this book is full of many of those scenarios. Unexpressed anger is just as destructive as expressed anger. Without voicing it, it will take up space in your mind until it makes you bitter, resentful, and difficult to be around, furthering your isolation. On the other hand, if expressed, it can bring deep emotional pain to all involved in a spontaneous and out-of-control outburst that is not easily mended. It can also terminate relationships.

We are responsible for the conversations we have at all times in our lives, including when we are grieving, struggling, or going through some other life crisis. I could not blame anyone but myself for the wrong things I listened to or took part in, and unfortunately, neither can you. It would be great if I could blame those who drew me in; but the truth is, I didn't need to respond, agree, or continuously rethink the things spoken.

Unfortunately, this kind of character maligning can be centered around many relationships, including the soon-to-be ex-spouse, the boss who fired you, the person who is deliberately destroying your reputation, God, and even your dead partner. I feel the pain of this because the kind of betrayal you will feel in some of these scenarios will make it difficult not to pay attention to the dirt that is being smeared. Emotional pain often seems to need a way to be vented for full healing, and it is essential. A few safer options may be to vent the emotion alone or within a safe group of people with similar experiences. Remember that there is a difference between the conversations that feed your pain and those that draw it out. One will make you bitter, while the other will help you heal.

The question remains: what do we do with the anger we feel? If you believe in and follow Jesus Christ, prayer is always the best place to begin. Continuing to be honest and vulnerable in your conversations with God will help you remove the power behind your anger. Don't be ashamed to go for professional help, though. Counseling, grief groups, divorce groups, and groups that help you determine the root of your anger can be very beneficial for anyone, Christian or not. In these environments, you will find yourself surrounded by a group of people who "get your pain," and that can be the beginning of your healing and the release of those pent-up emotions.

You do not walk your path alone; many are right where you are now, and they honestly "get you." Sitting in a room with these people enables you to be raw and honest because you will hear your pain from the voices of others as they share their experiences. These people speak your language, and they won't feel uncomfortable with what you say or the tears that won't stop. Look around your community to find what services and groups are provided and plug into one or more of them. Professional counselors can be expensive, but they can also be worth it when you find one you work well with. Finding one specializing in grief and trauma is worth the time it takes to search out. Finding facilities can easily be done by researching the internet or reaching out to family service centers in your area.

The important point in these suggestions is that I don't want you to spiral down into hopelessness, defeat, and crippling sorrow. I understand that this time and what you are going through is very overwhelming. However, among the many things you must take responsibility for, the one you have the most control over is yourself. Taking responsibility for your conversations during these harrowing experiences and forgiving those who have hurt you are two of the most freeing. I am not saying it won't be painful, but it will release you from other people's expectations.

Deciding whether and how to pursue your healing will be a daily decision for many months. While there is truth to the saying "Time heals all wounds," it is not completely accurate. The truth is, as time passes, the pain will become less intense, the tears will eventually stop, and you will once again return to some balance and joy in your life. You will be able to laugh again without guilt; but if you find yourself shying away from events, situations, or certain people, you likely have more work to do. You are responsible for your healing. You are responsible for looking fear, rage, grief, resentment, regret, and every "woulda, shoulda, coulda" in the face and depleting it of its power over you.

I use the term *lean into your pain*. When I use this phrase, I am not suggesting that you bury yourself in your agony and stop living. What I mean is, allow yourself to feel the pain, sorrow, and ache and experience it. Don't stuff it deep inside your heart just because it will be messy, and you want to appear in control because that might be the expectation put on you. Leaning into your pain can look like taking an entire day to sit on the couch and think about why you feel the way you do. Try to pinpoint what makes you so angry and then let it go. For example, if you feel like your anger is surfacing because someone in your inner circle keeps hijacking your decisions, I want to validate that. Take time to think about how you can respectfully speak up and take back your decision-making abilities. After all, it is your life. Then, feel the betrayal, resentment, or frustration. Let the emotions go after you have forgiven the individual for their part. It might help to visualize putting them in a boat or at the foot of the cross, handing them directly to Jesus and letting Him take them. Then, sit in the peace that comes afterward.

It is common for family members left behind to feel survivor's guilt. The questions of why you were allowed to live when your loved one died or why they had to get sick and die such an agonizing death while you remain topsoil and healthy are just two things you may need to work through. Survivor's guilt is very real, and no, it is not only experienced when a tragic accident or disaster occurs. Leaning into this false guilt is crucial. I struggled with this for some time because I felt like my husband was a much better, nicer person than

I was, plus he was two years younger. Why him? Genetics would also tell me that he should have outlived me by many, many years, except that isn't what happened. Leaning in to understand why you feel guilty that you are alive will help you deal with death and grief.

Being able to pinpoint this may reveal your insecurities and fears about yourself without your loved one and past occupation, abilities, income, support system, or identity. Revealing some of your "lean-in topics" can feel very uncomfortable and might trigger your "fight or flight" responses rather than give you a desire to lean into it. There can be a very awkward truth in recognizing that you allowed your identity to be wrapped up in another person, your career, your social position, or any other scenario that made you feel good about yourself.

I will admit that running away from unraveling the pain while ignoring the reality of our feelings is much easier than leaning into it. It can even seem like a reasonable solution until you have some of the loose ends tied up. However, if you find your relaxation and mind breaks in substances or things that can lead to addictions, please note that this will only numb the pain momentarily. It will not release it. There is never any healing at the bottom of a bottle. Yes, you may feel better for a moment; but the pain, grief, and remorse will return in full force at some point. Although much more socially acceptable, getting busy, staying busy, or being overcommitted has the same effect. Filling every waking moment so you don't have time to think or process your massive life shift will deplete you at the end of the day. Doing this will leave you unable to look deeply into your emotions, grief, or pain, which means they will remain untouched and left to fester.

Leaning into your feelings is the painful way to go; but it is also the most honest, helpful, and healing route. Being raw and honest with yourself and before God will make you whole again. If I can dare say it, I believe it can make you better! Doing this can make you a much better version of yourself.

Yes, you must acknowledge why you are feeling the emotions you are feeling but don't stay there. Forgive and release, forgive and release, forgive and release. Do it as often as you need to for everyone you must include. This list may include, but isn't limited to, yourself; the person who is the cause of your pain (ex-spouse, deceased loved one, or the one who ruined your reputation or gossiped about you and made you feel like you were doing it wrong); and maybe even God.

Leaning into your grief means acknowledging the loss you have suffered and the love you are missing. It means "owning" it and becoming OK with the fact that you hate it, that it hurts immensely, and that you have been forced to endure life this way. It is admitting you have some resentment for those around you who are enjoying what has been stolen from you. It means being honest with everything you feel. It will mean that you may look emotionally and perhaps physically messy and not put together, and it will probably mean more misunderstanding.

But it also means recognizing that you are responsible for finding the help you need so you can accept yourself and your new normal. No one can pick up the phone and make that call, make that appointment, or join a grief group but you! You must move past your pride or lack of courage that is preventing you from doing so. You must move past other people's expectations if you are going to be completely whole again. No other person can make you look at anything you don't want to see or deal with. Only you can do that.

I will end this chapter by stating that I want you to lean into your experience and bleed it dry. It does not need to own you. Bleed it dry. Use those tissues and get angry; but let it out in a safe space, in private, during counseling, or in the confines of a group of fellow travelers who understand you. Let those same people speak into your situation with their own experiences and heal together. It is worth the pain and the tears to have a heart that is free to love again and enjoy life once more. It is worth the pain and tears to be able and willing to embrace every experience that comes your way, both wanted and unwanted.

Time does not heal all wounds; but leaning into the experience—acknowledging, accepting, and owning how you feel—is the place to begin. Be raw, honest, and forgiving. Release those emotions that want to hold you to the event. Pray and invite Jesus Christ into your situation. Then, sit back and watch the miracle of emotional healing take place. It may take time, but it will happen, and it will be worth it.

Remember

For those in the struggle,

- We are responsible for what we say and how we respond to hurtful comments.
- Forgive, forgive, forgive.
- Try not to relive painful and wounding conversations.
- Not forgiving others will further your isolation and pain.
- Forgiveness allows you to heal.
- If the relationship is valuable to you, address the pain caused by the person.
- The grieving must take responsibility for their own actions and responses.
- Try not to get involved in conversations that put other people down.
- Don't meditate on negative things spoken to you about others.
- Remove yourself from negative conversations as quickly as you can for your health.
- Don't lash out.
- If you have a religious belief, pray.
- Don't be ashamed to go to a counselor or join a group.
- You are responsible for your healing.
- Lean into your pain and bleed it dry.
- Don't stuff your pain inside your heart.
- Don't turn to substances or busyness to numb the pain, or so you don't need to think about what has happened.

To the Supporters

- Do not silence the grieving.
- Massive life shifts create a huge loss of emotional, physical, financial, and sometimes spiritual instability.
- People can be emotionally hypersensitive while in emotional pain or grief.

CHAPTER 10

The Usual Well-Intended but Harmful Remarks

You may have already noticed that it doesn't matter what your difficult situation is; no shortage of insensitive comments will come your way. It is absurd when someone around you suggests that the intense pain and struggle you are going through are meant to make you a better person or teach you a much-needed lesson. The truth is we go through life, which can sometimes be messy and unpredictable.

A woman I was talking to had told me about her daughter's near-fatal car accident. In tears, she recounted the insensitive words spoken to her, suggesting that her suffering was meant to increase her compassion for others in pain. I was speechless. The mother before me took a deep breath and continued saying that she was then asked how it felt to be on the receiving end of the judgment of God. Uff da! All I could do was wrap my arms around her and cry with her. These were very damaging and unnecessary comments.

We all make mistakes and say things we would love to take back. Maybe this woman whose daughter had been injured had previously spoken things that had wounded others. I don't know, and I didn't ask. It is possible that she might have misspoken to the woman who said this to her at a previous time, who then took it as an opportunity to inflict painful remarks as a type of revenge. Again, I have no idea. What I do know is that these comments are a perfect example of what not to say.

As I walked through my pain and with others through theirs, there were some recurring "what not to say" moments. The following pages will contain some of the more common statements that resulted in intense emotional pain.

You Have Something to Learn

You have something to learn can also be framed as a question, "Do you have something to learn?" This can make this phrase sound more appealing and a little less harsh, but it does not remove the idea that the problem faced is the fault of the one going through it.

A couple had come to the house to pray with us around the midway mark of James's illness; as we were heading to the door, one turned to me and asked, "What do you think you are supposed to be learning?" My reply was that I didn't know. I wanted to ask what she thought I was supposed to be learning, but then again, did I want to know what she thought? That would likely cause more hurt and pain than the original question, so I left it.

I don't know *if* I was supposed to learn anything, and I don't know if I learned whatever I was supposed to learn even now. Had I learned it, would he have lived? Or was his death connected to the lesson? Was his death the thing I was to learn? Was I to learn how to be more compassionate, as stated to the woman whose daughter almost died? Was I supposed to learn to handle stress acceptably or maybe pray more? What was the reason for the "lesson"?

WHAT NOT TO SAY 177

What I came away with was that I don't control how long I or others will live, and it hurts so much when they die. In the same way, I cannot control my spouse's fidelity, thoughts, or actions. I recognize that it is very difficult when divorce is the result. It is a painful experience to realize that when the marriage vows were said, one person meant them; the other obviously did not. I cannot control the downsizing of the company I work at. Having to start a new career at fifty is terrifying, and the thoughts of failure and loss of things you own will keep you up at night. These are the things that I learned from my own experience and those of others who confided in me.

There are always things to learn, and we will learn new things on the journey we have to walk. The writing of this book would not have happened had I not gone through the struggles I endured. I can honestly say, however, that the writing of this book was not the reason I went through them. I did not need to watch my husband die so that I could address an issue that needed to be addressed for the betterment of us all. God is more significant than that! But I can also say He is using the things I went through for good.

What I speak next, I say as a Christian: I do not think that the God I serve is so limited in His power that He needs to begin to kill the people I love to get my attention. He is not so little in His ability that He needs to go to such extremes to teach us things. That is not who He is! I am not that hard-hearted or disobedient in my walk with God that He would need to resort to those measures, and more than likely, neither are you. My husband and my children were also not that indifferent or resistant to the things of God that He needed to get their attention this way. In much the same way, my husband did not get sick so that our extended family would begin to serve the Lord. The love of God is much more effective than the judgment of God when it comes to bringing change to those who call themselves by His name.

Now, did we learn things? Did I learn some things along the way? Absolutely! Did my children learn things? Of course, they did! Part of the reason for this is that we are created to learn from the things we go through, whether good or bad. When we had our first child, we learned how to parent effectively and how to put the needs of another (our son) above our own. We have learned much in our chosen fields of work. We learned about budgeting, living, traveling, and working out relationships every day. Each day, we learn how to communicate with others more effectively or how to voice concerns, opinions, and so much more. All these things are good, but they are also a part of living—a part of the journey of life! Yet in everyday events, including the very good, we are rarely asked, "What did you learn today?" even though, if we were to admit it, we learn the most in the everyday, mundane work-life, parenting, and relationship experiences. Why are we never asked this question after a routine day of life?

If you are a believer, I would ask how well you know the God you serve. If we believe God is a God of love who desires to do good things for His children and one who draws us close to Himself with His kindness, how can we believe simultaneously that He is so cold and harsh that He kills those we love to teach us something we refuse to learn otherwise? This statement, as well as the question, is absurd in so many ways! Either God is loving, kind, and compassionate, or He is not. But to imply that someone is going through what they are going through because it is the only way they will learn a valuable lesson is not helpful or encouraging. In truth, it is the opposite. It is hurtful and damaging and can make people question their relationship with God and others. It robs those it is spoken to of the ability to experience their emotions, as well as the precious moments they have left with their loved ones. It can cause doubts and fears that they or their loved ones are wrong, that they don't have a relationship with the Lord, that God is cruel, or that they are doing it wrong.

It Is for Your Good

A common and immensely harmful remark is "It is for your good." When this statement was said to me, I retorted with a harsh undertone, "How do you feel this will be good for me? In the long run, exactly how will this be good for me?" As shocking as it was to hear the statement, it seemed even more surprising to listen to the explanation: it was for my good because God wanted to move me into ministry, and I would now be free and unhindered to do so. Let me remind you that I was already in ministry when he got ill, and there was no reason to assume that I would stop because he was sick or died. He had been supportive and encouraging to me during the many years prior, and I had no reason to assume he would not continue to be. God didn't need to kill my husband so I could continue to do what I was already doing, even if it included a broader influence.

Let's look for the silver lining whenever we go through anything difficult. However, this is not a silver lining and should not be blurted out in conversation with someone who is aching because of loss. When we understand that God is our biggest and best cheerleader, we can begin to understand that although He does not kill the people around us, He will use it for our betterment if we allow Him to do so. In that sense, and with that understanding, we can agree with the statement "It is for your good." Yes, every problematic thing I go through will be used for my good because the God I serve is very, very good!

Think of the People You Will Be Able to Help

There have been times when I think back to the things said during, before, and after this part of my and my husband's lives; and I wonder why society thinks the way it does. Today, I reflect on the comment that "I would be able to help others" and receive it without feeling anything. At the time, however, I could not.

Let me share with you why I struggle with this statement. I was a victim of childhood sexual abuse, and I have heard others say that God allowed it to happen to them so that they could help other people in the same situation. For the record, I have never accepted this statement to be true.

Once again, I do not think that the God of love that I serve sits in heaven and *lets* little boys and girls be raped, fondled, or otherwise damaged so that He will one day be able to use it to "help someone else in the same situation"! No, the God I serve is big and powerful enough to protect those being abused and end childhood sexual abuse, and He does not want this to happen to any innocent person. "But whoever causes one of these little ones who believe and trust in Me to stumble [that is, to sin or lose faith], it would be better for him if a heavy millstone [one requiring a donkey's strength to turn it] were hung around his neck and he were thrown into the sea" [Mark 9:42 AMP]. Can you see by the reference I used how ludicrous this statement sounds? If we look around, listen to the news, or talk deeply with a few of those around us, we can quickly see the effects of evil men and women all around us. Then, if we are willing to acknowledge that evil exists and embodies human beings, we can understand why awful things happen.

It can be comments like this that make me want to question, "Do you hear yourself? Did you consider the words you said before you said them? Do you believe what you said or what you implied? Is that the God you serve?" The truth is that I have led many courses and groups on healing the trauma of childhood sexual abuse, and yes, those courses did help those in the group. But that is not why I was sexually abused! If God is big enough to heal the wound of it, He is certainly big enough to stop it from happening in the first place.

Comments like this show that we feel we must have answers for everything, regardless of how nonsensical the things we say are or irrespective of how hurtful and damaging the effects are on the people we tell them to. I believe we are born with the need to make sense of the senseless and painful things around us, but we cannot always do so. We need to categorize and put pain in some order that will eventually bring happiness to us so that we can function in our lives. If we don't look further than the surface, we will always need to come up with a reason, a lesson, or a cure that satisfies an unwanted and uncomfortable problem or puts an end to that problem. There is a concerning barrier with this way of thinking: there is not always a reason, a lesson, or a cure for every problem we face. Sometimes, it is just the way life goes.

Many of the statements I have mentioned in this book are spoken to people regardless of their faith walk or lack of faith. Please

WHAT NOT TO SAY

understand that what you are going through will change you, but you are not going through it because you need to be changed. Whether you have faith or love Jesus, life struggles come; and when they do, you will learn many things. Yes, you will likely become more compassionate, but that is *not* why you go through them.

We are all born, live our lives, and then we die. While alive, we will experience the joy of birthing our children or watching others we are close to. We will have high points, low points, celebrations, and sorrows. We will all experience the mundaneness of everyday life. Then, as life goes by, we will experience the death of those we hold dear and, one day, our own. I know that sounds morbid, but it is still valid. After we die, those people who loved us will mourn, and they will struggle for a while because they loved us. We will all experience these things, but we will also choose how and what to do with the things that cross our paths.

It is nobody's fault! What you are suffering through is not a lesson to be learned. It is not so that you can write a book or help someone else. It is also not because it is the only way God can get your attention. It is because we are living in a fallen world. We are accepting life with all its ups and downs, highs and lows, loves and losses, mountains and valleys, celebrations and sorrows. It is up to us to deal with life as it happens.

Lean in and experience whatever place in life you find yourself. Every part of your life has the potential to make you a more rounded, compassionate, loving, and gentle person and draw you closer to God. Remember, if you know Jesus, He is the great comforter. He is always waiting to meet you wherever you are and in whatever you are going through.

Suppose you don't know Jesus Christ as your personal Lord and Savior and want to invite Him into your life and pain. Please pray this prayer:

> Jesus Christ, I acknowledge that my current situation overwhelms me. I feel like a failure, and I know that

> I have done many things that make me feel like you would want nothing to do with me. I am a sinner far from You in my heart, mind, and actions.
>
> I ask you to forgive me right now for everything I have ever done that was displeasing to you. I invite you to come in and clean up my heart and my life. Please give me your peace, your security, and your love.
>
> Thank you, Jesus, for hearing me, for receiving me, and for loving me!

If you prayed this prayer for the first time, I encourage you to find a Bible-believing Christian church and begin attending. Also, start talking to Jesus daily through praying and reading your Bible. (Your phone and computer have Bible apps that are easy to use and come complete with devotionals.)

Remember

For Those Supporting

- Don't assume that the difficulties a person is going through are because they need to learn something.
- Remember, God is a good Father who loves and desires to do good things for His children, not kill their families.
- God is not limited in His abilities, so He does not need to harm people to get the glory.
- There isn't always a reason, a lesson, or a cure.

For the Caregiver, Sick, or Hurting

- You are not going through trials so you can help someone else in the future.

CHAPTER 11

Grief

We have explored many things throughout the pages of this book. Although not exhaustive by any means, it is an excellent beginning to unwrapping the complexities of knowing what to say, how to help, and how to walk with deeply hurting people.

Understand that being awkward around the hurting is not an isolated incident. It does happen to almost everybody. It is also OK that you don't know what to say, feel confused, and don't know what to do when you see your friend in tears. All this is fine! It is even expected. When you find yourself in this situation, express to the person in front of you that words escaped you, and you have no idea what to say or do because you don't want to make it worse. Explaining your awkwardness does help to remove some of the strangeness from the situation. To be completely honest, the person across the table from you, or standing in front of you, does not know what they need from you, either. The awkwardness goes both ways.

It would not be fair of me to tell you to try to put yourself in their shoes. If you have never experienced a similar loss, you will be unable to do so. The kinds of life experiences you have had will either help you find a position of connection and empathy or leave you scrambling to understand. There are many life trials outside of the realm of our personal experience that make it difficult to address many issues successfully. But we can listen! We can ask questions, we can meet the needs they have, and we can pray for them if you do that sort of thing. What we should not do is try to "fix it." We should also not try to find the "reason" behind the suffering, and we should definitely not add to the anger that they might be feeling. Anger only sometimes needs to be validated because it can feed it and make it grow.

If you are still trying to figure out what to do, listening is a beautiful and safe place to begin. It brings much more support and healing than you may be aware of. Ensure you listen with intention and engage your heart to the pain being expressed. Be ready with a box of tissues and a trash bin and be the shoulder to cry on. This might seem uncomfortable to you, and you may feel awkward doing it, but retelling the story and releasing the pain brings a healthy outlet that invites eventual healing.

The truth is, you may be required to listen more than once to the same story; please, let them tell it anyway. One book I read in the first year of losing my husband had some beneficial tips. I decided to put my wholehearted effort into one in particular. The condensed version and my takeaway was to bleed it dry. As I continued to think about what was said, I realized that one of the things I needed to do was to bleed the death scene dry so that it held no power over me, didn't keep me awake at night, and didn't scramble my thinking when it surfaced. Sounds rough? It was.

You see, I was also going to bed each evening with the foreboding thought that when I closed my eyes, I would relive James's final hours one more time. I knew it needed to be done. Bleeding it dry meant I would need to look at those last hours of James's life, intentionally relive it, and consciously feel all the feelings. Furthermore, I knew I would need to look this deeply into it until it was no longer painful or searing a path through my brain during countless sleepless nights. Doing this would mean that I would also need to unleash the memories of the little beads of moisture on his head and hear the death rattle echoing through my soul. And that sound was one I would have given anything to stop from happening, and yet, the only way that was going to happen was if I "bleed it dry."

It felt torturous every time I let the memories surface and remain surfaced. I did it, though, and I did it intentionally. In doing it, it eventually became nothing more than a memory that is no longer painful or one that I want to avoid. But I would like to say a deep, meaningful thank you to those who listened to me as I cried my way through the retelling. You helped me heal, and I am grateful.

While you sit with others, feel free to ask questions pertinent to the telling of their story, which will help release the sorrow and pain of what they are going through. Ask them to tell you what happened, "Can you tell me the story?" Just don't rush or push them if they cannot give all the details; that may come later. Ask them how they are, and then let them tell you. Do not tell them they should be feeling differently. Be attentive when they speak, and do not argue or give advice when they share how they are feeling or what they are doing.

One of the things that happened far too often was the rundown of questions, "How are you? How is his mom? How are the kids?" While these questions are OK, please don't jump too quickly to ask how everyone else in the family is handling the loss or crisis, especially if they are not in the room. Give time for a complete response because when you quickly jump to others who have been affected, you minimize the experience of the person in front of you. Instead, minister to your friend one-on-one and be interested in every word they say, even if you feel out of your comfort zone. Doing this validates their pain, loss, feelings, and experience. Remember, *this is about them!*

As they tell their story, ask questions that bring more clarity to their experiences, such as the following:

- How many times was he admitted to the hospital in total?
- Why did you feel like it was more than strep throat?
- How did you feel when the blood disease specialist told you there was nothing they could do?

Encouraging someone while removing the awkwardness you feel because you are afraid you will mess up is as simple as listening to the answers they give. Respond with a heartfelt

- Wow, that sounds like it was very challenging. I am sorry.
- No wonder you are exhausted.
- I can understand why you were afraid.
- I think you are doing well, considering what you have just gone through.

Remember

- It is OK to tear up and even cry with your hurting friend.
- It is OK to be silent.
- It is OK not to have an answer!

Always let them lead the conversation. If they don't want to discuss it, that is OK too. If they are willing and want to share, let them go as deep or as shallow as possible. If they begin to recognize you as a safe place for them to share, cry, and be upset, it may enable them to become more honest and vulnerable in the future.

Take the time to pray for them when you are at home alone; pray for them whenever you think of them; and, most importantly, pray for them while you are with them if they are open to it. Prayer in person is underestimated and should be acted upon every chance you are given. If you are not a person of prayer, or perhaps neither of you is a believer, end your time with words that comfort and encourage them, but don't minimize their situation. Maybe say things along the following lines:

- I am so grateful that you allowed me a small window into the things you have gone through.
- That could not have been easy for you to tell me, but I am so thankful you did.
- I want you to know that I will not retell your story. That is reserved for you.
- I will bring you a meal tomorrow. Would that be OK? Would it work for you if I drop it off at 5:00 p.m.?

One of the most common statements is "Just let me know if you need anything." This is not helpful for several reasons. They probably don't know what they need, and it can be very difficult to ask. May I suggest you ask something along these lines:

- Can I cut your lawn on Thursdays after I cut mine?
- I'm out grocery shopping tomorrow. What do you need?
- Would you like to come along? I will call before I leave.
- I see you have a (specific need), and I would like to do that for you.

Sometimes, people who are hurting don't want to feel like they are an inconvenience, so let them off the hook. Instead of asking if they would like a meal, let them know you have made too much and you would like to drop it off for them. This still allows them to decline while enabling you to meet a need if they accept.

People going through the wringer don't want to feel like an obligation that must be fulfilled, so I hope you found some of these suggestions helpful. I also hope that what I have mentioned will help you feel less awkward and self-conscious so that you can feel comfortable enough to be a support person without much second-guessing or beating yourself up. I understand how uncomfortable some of what I have written may feel to many of you. Remember, you are not there to fix, heal, or change them. Your job, if you want to call it that, is to love them exactly where they are. I promise you that will be enough.

There seems to be a concern from many people who are friends or family of those mourning that they will be forever stuck in a place of grief or pain from the death of a loved one, their painful and devastating divorce, or some other loss. I want to acknowledge that that sometimes happens, but it is also important not to place your expectations for healing and recovery onto them, especially in the first three to five years.

I have only met a few people since my husband passed who have gotten stuck in their pain and loss, but they also knew it. They were able to verbalize that they were bogged down and couldn't get past the event, but each person I encountered was over the ten-year mark in their journey. Try not to be overly concerned about your loved one as long as they are progressing slowly in the right direction.

Remember, Grief Is a Reality, Not a Figment of Your Imagination

Where are you on your journey? You may have just entered the battlefield of hardship and pain, or maybe you have been here for a while already. Please be considerate of your scattered thinking because it will be that way for a while. In the beginning stages of any loss, your thoughts are often linked to shock. The circumstances around that loss won't limit the effects of shock, even when expected. It is challenging to comprehend the loss of someone you loved, and wrapping your head and heart around the events of that traumatic time is not easy.

When I think back to my journey, I knew my husband would die because he had aggressive acute myeloid leukemia and did not qualify for a stem-cell transplant. Yet in the days following his death, I was still in shock that he had died! I walked around in a daze. I couldn't think, eat, sleep, read, pray, focus, or sometimes complete my sentences. Sitting on the loveseat, I realized I would meet our first biological grandchild alone in less than six months. Loss. Tears streamed down my face as other dreams slowly surfaced and disappeared like bubbles in the wind. Just like his life, they just ended. There was no lifeline to continue because half of the equation was gone. In all the years we had been married, this was a scenario that I had never anticipated. I was ill prepared for it and had no idea what I was doing. This was not how it was supposed to be.

Not real! That was the best way to describe how I felt in those first days. Unreal! My heart and mind screamed that this was very, very wrong, somehow. And why on earth was my neighbor cutting his lawn? The everyday activities of everyone else's lives came crashing into my world of devastation with an incredible and unyielding inability to mesh the two. I was very aware of what had happened, and yet I was unable to accept that things kept moving forward for others. Surreal!

Grief is a reality that really challenges you in the most unpleasant ways. Your grief may be "haunted" by a last conversation, argument, look, event, or memory. Why? Although you might not have known it then, this was the final goodbye. In your attempt to bring closure to what was the end, you will likely replay that timeframe repeatedly in your mind, burning the image into your memory. For me, this event was the last moment of his life: the death rattle, the little beads of sweat on his forehead, the smell in the room, and my fast-beating, fearful heart. I wanted to be anywhere on earth but in that room, while at the same time, there was nowhere else I would rather be. I could close my eyes for months afterward and relive that memory in detail. Haunted! Death can be traumatic.

As those first months passed, the agony deepened. The grief bursts left me emotionally and physically depleted, each one leaving me wondering if I would be able to take the next breath. I had no idea you could grieve so deeply that it seemed like every bit of oxygen had left your lungs while still expelling more until I experienced it. I quickly found that sleepless nights are to be expected and that broken heart syndrome is a real thing, and it is rough. Yes, grief is unbearable and tormenting in many ways, and sometimes you don't want to wake up in the morning. Once again, I say grief is hard.

But you will find your way. You may not feel like you are doing well. On some days, you won't be, but you will do better than you think you are doing just because you are doing it. You will learn to live your life once again after you have struggled with, wrestled, and killed your giants. Overcoming the hurdles placed before you may seem unscalable at times. But understand that they can. You will figure it out, but you will also trip over or bump into them as well. You will likely put too much pressure on yourself to heal faster than is reasonable, so I encourage you to take your time because healing takes time. Never push anything under the carpet because those around you don't understand. Doing that will only lead to complications later when you are caught off guard by an eruption of emotions from within you that seem to come from nowhere.

Three and a half years after my husband's death, I found myself being very distracted. I was unable to retain information or complete simple tasks. It wasn't until the end of the day, when I was writing in my gratitude journal, that I realized why I had the day I did. It was our wedding anniversary. I was proud of myself, though. Although no one else understood, and even I wasn't sure why, I allowed myself to feel what I felt. After I realized what was happening, I experienced ten days where I found sleeping difficult. I didn't cry; I wasn't even sad, but I was remembering, so I journaled and prayed. When will it end? I have no idea. Perhaps it will never entirely end because I will never forget him. As I say to our kids, "There will always be a James-sized hole in my heart."

You do not need to feel ashamed of your grief; therefore, it is worth the effort to work against the expectations that others will place on you to speed up the process. Your grief will make others uncomfortable, but that doesn't mean you need to hide it or put on a happy face to make them comfortable. That is not your job! Your sole job at the moment is to walk through the healing process one step at a time. Congratulate yourself each day you make it through because, at the beginning of your journey, that goal is big enough to consume most of your energy.

Grief is real and is as uniquely felt as each individual who goes through it. I will not tell you that you are doing it wrong simply because there is no wrong way of doing it. I will also not ask you to speed up the process because I was not part of the relationship you lost. I cannot understand your pain. I can tell you this one thing: you are doing it! You will wake up in the morning and go to bed in the evening. You may sleep, and you may not. You may be able to get tasks completed, and you may not. You may eat, and you may not, but you will probably cry.

I can also tell you this: one day, you will wake up and feel something you have not felt for a very long time. It may take some time to figure out what it is, but one day, you will wake up and feel *hope*. That is a good sign, my friends! It means you are coming through. Enjoy that day and the hours you feel *hope* in your soul because it will flit in and out of your life for many days, weeks, and months before it takes up permanent residency again.

You are on a journey that you did not bargain for. You are not losing your mind. You are not permanently broken; you are grieving the loss of something or someone very dear to you. You are suffering because you loved, and that is precious. Don't ever lose that, and please don't hide it! If we can rejoice and remember with fondness the wedding, the birth of children, the promotions, and the accolades of life, then we must also be free to sorrow the loss of the same.

Remember

For Those Supporting

- Listening is always a great place to start.
- Let them tell the story and let them tell it as often as they need to.
- Ask them to tell the story.
- Ask questions that will help them to tell their story.
- It is OK to get emotional and weep or tear up with your friend as they tell their story.

For the Grieving

- Progressing slowly through the pain is a marker of recovery.
- It may feel like you can't jump the hurdles before you, but in time, you will.
- Don't feel ashamed of your grief.
- Your current job is to walk through the healing process one step at a time.
- You will wake up one day and feel something you haven't felt for a very long time: hope.

CHAPTER 12

Things that Ease the Pain

Throughout this book, we have discussed many difficulties in extreme situations that leave us grieving. Regardless of what brought you to this book, no matter your loss, I hope you have found some nuggets of truth that will help you through your journey. I understand that some of the things you may have faced probably came out of left field. You found yourself reeling in disbelief and shock, and there was nothing you could have done to change your circumstances or the outcomes you found yourself in.

Life doesn't come with warning labels, making it very difficult to be emotionally prepared for some of the significant life changes that may come your way. Here are a few examples of unexpected massive shifts: the affair you found your spouse in, a divorce you weren't expecting, disease and illness, the job or career loss that ripped your world apart, as well as many others. It is hard to be prepared for things you hope will never happen. You may do your best to live in a way that hopefully prevents these things from happening, but that is the best you can do.

There is a difference, however, with the death and dying process. These two life events will happen to everyone, but they also have some unique preparations that help ease the process a little for you. I don't know where you stand on issues like predeath planning, wills, or life insurance; but I encourage you to take the time to consider what I am about to write. Please don't skip this chapter!

Let's embark on the three big avoiders: life insurance, wills, and predeath planning. As human beings, most of us like to avoid the things that make us the most uncomfortable. Undoubtedly, considering our own death has got to be at the top of that list. What we try to do with our mortality is sidestep the inevitable, even though we know that "no one gets out alive." We avoid things that make us think about death, especially our own or those around us that we love the most. I will give you my insights as to why I believe that life insurance, wills, and predeath planning are essential to have in place. As a believer in Jesus Christ, I believe He led my husband and me to complete all three because He profoundly loves us. I must say that I am incredibly thankful that we were obedient to do what He was requiring us to do.

Life Insurance

Many months before my husband's heart attack, I began to feel the need to get good life insurance. What I mean when I say that is that we needed to find a good, stable company that followed through with life insurance monies. I know that this may sound like a ridiculous statement, but knowing that they are not equal is necessary and very beneficial. Some life insurance companies will look for a caveat so they don't need to pay the whole portion upon death. This could very easily have been the case with my husband, seeing that he had his heart attack days after the final signing of the documents. I don't want to alarm you (OK, maybe I do), but it is true nevertheless. Finding out which company will benefit you the most will require some research. You don't want to find yourself spending thousands of dollars through the years only to be getting next to nothing when you need it the most.

Before James's heart attack, I began to feel the need to get life insurance. I attribute this feeling to the Lord because there was no other reason for it. We were young and healthy. We had no concerns of any kind, but almost a year before his heart event, I began to experience a gentle nudging that this was what we needed to do. As time progressed, this gentle nudging turned into me waking up in the night in a cold sweat, panicking that we must get it done.

My husband was not interested at first, and when he asked me why I felt the way I did, I had no explanation other than I thought it was God prompting us to do it. He was avoidant, but I was persistent, and he finally agreed. Signing the final documents for the life insurance gave me peace and rest for a very short time. Only days after the signing took place, James had his heart attack at the age of forty-eight. We had done our research, and we had a good life insurance company that acknowledged that the papers had been signed and ensured us that the policy remained intact without discrepancy. There were also no amendments to or cancellations of the policy because of recent and sudden developments.

Many life insurance policies can and often will use scenarios like this to cancel your policy, but the one we had chosen honored the signing and the previous medical exams. We were beyond grateful. Another thing to take notice of is that once you have a heart attack or have been found with a terminal illness, you no longer qualify for benefits. We made it under the wire. I remember my oldest son calling the agent while we were waiting for James to get out of surgery, letting him know what had just transpired and inquiring whether they would honor the contract. What a relief to find out they considered it legal and binding upon signature.

During the life insurance application process, we decided to get a "rider" on our policy, which enabled us to withdraw some of the money if he or I became terminally ill. Again, we had no idea when we signed these papers that my husband would shortly have a heart attack and that he would be deceased three and a half years later. We had no idea that we had been given such a small window of opportunity and that he had such a short time to live. When my husband became terminally ill with acute myeloid leukemia just fifteen months after his heart attack, we withdrew some cash from the insurance policy. This enabled us to purchase a new vehicle and do a little "bucket list" traveling. After James died, the life insurance allowed me to stay at home and do the grieving I needed to do. It gave me options. It allowed me to pay for the funeral without doing a GoFundMe. We didn't have a significant policy, but it was enough to help me get my feet back under me without worrying about finances.

I understand that life insurance is a monthly bill that can sometimes feel like an unnecessary burden on an already-strained pocketbook. But had we not had it, my life would have looked much different today. Not to mention that the funeral cost would have added unnecessary stress to an already-taxing time. Having this in place left me with a sense of peace I would not have otherwise. For us, the monthly cost of life insurance policies was worth it. The following paragraphs will help you determine the best policy for you. A trusted professional in the industry writes it:

> There is a realization when someone passes that two deaths occur: the first—physical, the second—financial. If anyone is dependent on your income, life insurance is essential.
>
> If you currently have life insurance, do you know
>
> —What type you have?
>
> —If you are being overcharged and under-protected?
>
> If you don't have it yet, do you know
>
> —How much you require to cover your unique needs and budget? There may be mortgage payments, daycare costs, education savings, living expenses, etc., for the family left behind.

—How long those needs would need to be taken care of?

As not all insurance companies are the same, experts agree that individually-owned term policies are the best choice, and I agree. It can seem overwhelming when researching and choosing the right life insurance company. A small percentage of companies will meet superior ratings, and you want to look for factors such as payment of claims track record, length of term to cover your needs and not be faced with increased premium renewal rates, outstanding customer service, and the company's reputation.

This policy will be your personal and final communication (I've been told and like to refer to the policy as your 'Love Letter') to your family. What do you want to say to them? How do you want to assist them financially to cover any burdens you may leave behind?

Do you want to leave a legacy or inheritance for them? Is your "Love Letter" written?

It may be because of my story, but I am an avid supporter and advocate for having life insurance. My only regret is that we hadn't started sooner. Life insurance becomes more expensive the older you get and is more difficult to obtain as your health deteriorates. It is easy to think that it won't happen to me. However, it will happen to all of us at one time or another; and if you are prepared, your preplanning will speak volumes to those left behind. As my friend and trusted professional said, it is your last love letter to your family. I found it very accurate.

Wills

We determined to get our wills in place after James had his heart attack. The wake-up call made us aware that our today is not promised to us, so we should be as prepared as possible. I am not saying we took a doom-and-gloom approach to our lives because we did not. We still had faith, loved God, and served Him faithfully. We still believed we would grow old together and live out our days enjoying our family. In fact, after James recovered, we were exceptionally grateful and filled with joy because we had a testimony of the goodness of God.

Our lives had been altered, though, and we understood that life is fragile. Therefore, it would be a good idea to get everything in place as soon as possible for some time in the distant future. As we already had the life insurance in place and had come through the heart attack, we determined that making the will was the next logical step. We were not wealthy, but we did want the little we had to get into the hands of the people we wanted it to go to.

Without a will, how your assets will be distributed will be determined by the province (in Canada) where you live. Your wishes for your loved ones are not considered. If it is important that the ones you leave behind are recipients of your possessions and money, please take the time to create a will. Yes, it can feel awkward and even a bit morbid, perhaps, but once again, your family will be thankful for it. There can be delays and extra expenses that eat away at the little you have if you do not have a will.

Often, all that is needed is a copy of the first page of the will stating that you, as the spouse, have been left as the estate's sole beneficiary. This allows you to continue to live in your home, access all bank accounts, pay off debts, keep personal property, and distribute things as was indicated by the deceased. It also gives you the right to receive any work-related insurance your spouse may have been entitled to. Most Canadian adults don't have a signed will. Did you know that if you die without a valid will or if your will can't be found, all your assets and liabilities go into a separate legal entity called your estate? The living spouse or family can only access its contents once the government has settled the estate. Imagine the stress level this can add to the grieving, not to mention financial difficulties.

We made our appointment and went to Edmonton to talk to the lawyer. It seemed odd, yes, but we decided to make the best of the day to help relieve some of the awkwardness of it. We went for lunch, went to the appointment, and then sat at an outdoor coffee shop on Whyte Avenue, where we enjoyed coffee and a delicious dessert. Knowing that we live in a society where we want the fast-food drive-through experience to be a constant in almost everything we do, we found that this process took us longer than we thought it would.

Deciding who would get what was one thing and seemed to be the easy part, but we found that there were many other things to be considered. During the preparation of the will, we were first introduced to the idea of considering what we wanted for end-of-life care for ourselves and each other. This generated some interesting conversations, to be sure. Making your will may make you uncomfortable, and that is OK. Do it anyway. You will be glad you did, and so will your family.

We need to get over only being comfortable with our grandparents or elderly parents making a will and discussing their desires for their possessions while avoiding the same conversations and precautions ourselves. We would never consider getting married, having a baby, or buying a house without being prepared. In the same manner, we should consider the end of life as significant as the beginning and all the celebratory moments in between. Being prepared means loving those left behind, which means taking care of them in significant, intentional, and thoughtful ways.

The will we had done included end-of-life care, and to be completely transparent, we struggled through the decisions that needed to be made. But I can tell you that when my husband could not verbalize any longer, and the doctors needed to know what he wanted, I could articulate his desires, knowing I was speaking for him after

I handed them the living will. There was tremendous comfort in having discussed it with him and having it written down and signed as a legal document. Even though it felt raw and unpleasant at the time, it alleviated questions and removed responsibility from me or our kids when needed most.

I cannot say that I did not cry or that I could even get the words from my mouth, but I did have his living will with me, and I could hand it over. No one wants to look a doctor in the eye when their loved one is in critical condition and make those decisions or say the words, "There is to be no resuscitation of any kind." I cannot stress enough how this one uncomfortable act will alleviate the guilt from your family for having to make the call.

Preplanning the Funeral

This step is the last of the big three. It is no less uncomfortable, painful, or exhausting than the others. It means looking at your life and how you lived and making decisions regarding your death and the final celebration of you. What do you want? How do you want people to remember you? What do you want to focus on? What songs do you want to be sung? And would you rather be buried or cremated?

I can sense your discomfort as I write the words on the page, but this is another way to tell those around you that you love them enough to ease some of this burden. I recognize that this may not always be possible. In the case of a sudden, unexpected death of a healthy loved one because of a car crash or some other tragedy, the family will be left to plan without knowing your requests.

Both my husband and my brother Eric would look me in the eye and say, "I never thought I would be planning my own funeral." Unfortunately, they were placed in that position, but they did it. I sat with them both and wrote down their decisions regarding the songs, scriptures, facilitators, pallbearers, cremation, and all the rest. This selfless and uncomfortable act on their part enabled me and my brother's fiancée to ensure they got what they wanted—nothing more and nothing less. If it was possible, it was done; if it was not what they wanted, it did not happen.

Funeral homes have predeath planning kits, and a funeral director will sit with you and gently and compassionately help you wade through the many decisions that need to be made. They understand that you would rather not be doing this. You may be emotionally and physically taxed or angry, and you will probably feel a lot of things, but they are very skilled at what they do. By letting them help you, you are pulling on a professional resource that will enable you and your family to worry less when it is the most difficult for you. There is, of course, a fee for this; but in my opinion, it is well worth the cost to ensure that the last wishes are met. Even when all this was finished, I still needed to make decisions, but I am thankful that James had taken care of the more extensive details.

Conclusion

I am uncertain what it is precisely that causes us to avoid making these preparations. You are not being morbid in taking these steps. It does not mean you have no faith or believe God will not care for you. Instead, it makes you a responsible person. It may, and probably will, feel awkward, especially if you do so when you are young and healthy; but remember whom you are doing it for. You are doing this first for yourself, so love yourself enough to prepare for your legacy. Then, remember you are doing it as an act of love for your family.

Looking at the end of our existence on earth can seem so final if we do not understand that there is an eternity waiting for us after our last breath here on this earth. The belief that this is all there is to our lives and that we have just a few short years before we stop existing, of course, makes the prospect of our death that much more difficult to accept. Being uncertain of your destination is also a valid reason not to want to look at the end of our lives. What do you believe? Why do you believe it? In the last chapter, I will write a short explanation of why I believe as I do and include a prayer if you want to be sure of your salvation and life after death.

It has been my experience that although we would like to think that death, dying, and funerals bring out the best in people, the opposite is often true. It can bring out the worst and often does. When my parents died, it was suggested that we put all their belongings in six even piles, one for each child, so the distribution was fair and equal. Not only was this impossible, but it was also not what my parents wanted. Thank goodness they had a will, and therefore, the distribution of their possessions could not be contested.

One of the most significant decisions you will be required to make will be that of burial or cremation. This is also one that others will most often challenge. Regardless of which of these two options you choose, there will be those who disagree with your decision. Is cremation wrong for Christians? I believe this is a personal choice and not one that keeps a person out of the kingdom of heaven. I do not think Jesus would consider this a deal-breaker for salvation. It has been the traditional way for many people to bury their dead through the years. Cremation can be significantly less expensive, which is often why many choose this option; but it has no significant spiritual effect, in my opinion.

I want to stress that the three giants mentioned in this section are all business related, and the businesses are out to do what companies do, and that is to make money. Make sure you shop around to get the best results for the least cost because the difference, unfortunately, can be thousands of dollars out of your pocket. Like all businesses, some are more attentive to client's needs than others, and you will find the right person or establishment you relate to best. We all know how important that can be in any situation, but in circumstances of this magnitude, the people you deal with can be like gold to you. That is what you will need, my friend, not more stress.

CHAPTER 13

Where I Am Now

When I first considered writing this book, it was an overwhelming project. I was unsure if I would ever be emotionally prepared to write it. Yet here I am! Writing a book on experiences that my family and I have gone through has been a roller coaster of emotions that has somehow brought an avalanche of healing! My boys both mentioned to me how they felt all the feelings resurface as they wrote and broke down in tears as their memories poured onto the pages, as did I when I read what they had written. But like me, they both felt tremendous relief and healing when they were done. Sometimes, it just needs to come out.

Since September 9, 2017, we have been on a long and winding journey with many struggles, emotions, and pain. We have all grown tremendously and healed significantly. I was able to come to a place where I could choose to love again and take the chances that go with it. I am stronger in many ways and have discovered things about myself that I either never knew existed or had buried many years ago. Perhaps I had forgotten that I am those things too. I can see the good stuff inside of me now because I was willing to trudge through the swamp to heal.

I love reading, writing, studying God's Word, and teaching. From this love of digging into the Word of God, I continue to lead and write Bible studies so that we can all grow, learn, and appreciate everything written in God's love letter to us! This love and desire to know His Word has brought me to create a blog, which can be accessed on YouTube under *Cheryl Bay*. The podcast on YouTube is *The Offering*, and you can also find me on cheryloutten7.blogspot.ca. The blog includes many topics besides grief (although you may find that occasionally), as well as prayer videos and much more.

Being the associate pastor at Fireplace Church in Stony Plain, where I preached frequently, I was also blessed to have led and built various studies. I constructed a prayer study guide that I taught for three consecutive years in the church, which equips others to become trained and confident in their ability to pray in a public gathering and in private. The study explores everything from list prayers to creative prayer models. I desire to see those within these groups become strong prayer warriors and leaders who pray and lead prayer meetings, especially the young. I hope for a movement of prayer that will cover the globe, with each person walking prophetically and submitting to the will and purposes of God as they do so. This passion has led me to attend, lead, and encourage others in prayer meetings in Calgary, Alberta, as well as on Zoom after my second marriage, where I continue to implement this teaching and freedom in prayer.

Working in prayer counseling for many years, I am always incredibly blessed to hear the life stories of so many and pray with them toward healing. One of the greatest gifts I can give is a listening ear and an open heart, embracing and loving people in difficult situations. What an incredible privilege and honor I have been given.

My experiences have placed within me a longing to see people accepted and loved during the difficult times of life. More than anything, I want to give the brokenhearted their voice back so that they do not feel like they need to hide their sorrow and their pain, which can cripple, distort, and delay their healing process. If I can make the difficult road of life's most unbearable moments easier to travel for even a few people, I will have completed my mission well. But to be honest, I desire much more than that.

You see, I desire a time when no one needs to hide behind a smile on a face that means nothing more than a self-protective act to shield a shattered heart. I desire for all of us to give voice to our pain and be accepted while doing it. I want healing for these same wounded men and women rather than the shame and guilt placed upon already heavily burdened shoulders because they feel they aren't doing it right! I would love to extinguish false expectations on how to handle and display emotionally tricky moments.

I would love to remove false expectations that say humans cannot mourn, be depressed, face life-altering events, be ill, or struggle. Life happens to us all, and so does death. The belief system that says "We should receive only good things" is broadly accepted in many circles of belief, both religious and nonreligious. However, it is inaccurate because not one of us controls our tomorrows.

In Matthew 14, we see the disciples in a boat in the middle of a storm. It is easy to focus on the part of the story where Peter gets out of the boat and walks on the water. In his inability to keep his eyes focused on Jesus Christ, he begins to sink and, in the sinking, calls out to the Lord for help. We can look at this story and say, "Oh, Peter, you of little faith." But let me remind you that Peter got out of the boat during a storm so large it threatened to take his life!

During the storm, Peter walked on the very thing he was most afraid of, and he walked with his Lord when he did so. He could never have overcome or put the thing he feared under his feet if he had stayed in the boat or on the shore. Jesus knew this, and it might be why we see in verse 22 that Christ *made* them get into the boat and go to the other side. Jesus made his disciples enter the boat, knowing full well that this massive storm was coming. How does that fit into what we believe?

The storms of life will come, but knowing who controls the storm will help you remain faithful and overcome your fears. Just like the disciples, you will always be safer in the middle of the storm when in the will of God rather than out of the will of God and on the shore, where, in many ways, it appears safer. This may be a controversial and perhaps unappreciated look at a familiar portion of scripture, but it doesn't make it less accurate. Jesus desires that we be submissive, obedient children at all times and in all circumstances.

It may be because of my own experiences, but I like to listen to people tell their stories and encourage them as they go through hard things. I now know that I don't need to have all the answers and that it is best if I don't. I can also only talk from my experience. I understand that my experience may not speak to yours, but it is nevertheless "my story," just as your story is yours and is equally as powerful. I would like to encourage us with that thought in mind to fully embrace the life experiences and faith journeys we will all go through.

My final thought here is this, and the advice I have to give is to live life in color! You never know when a sore throat will change your life!

Who Is Jesus?

You have heard a little about my story in the few pages of this book, and I try to live my life in such a way that Jesus Christ is my everything. I was raised in a minimally Christian home, but I heard Jesus audibly tell me to give my life to Him when I was just days shy of turning twenty-three years old. We have walked together since that time, and I have been better for it each and every day. I am not perfect, and I have made many mistakes along the way. But He is faithful and forgiving and has always received me and continued to love me.

You may wonder who this Jesus Christ is that I have fallen in love with. Let me explain. He is the only Son of God, conceived by the Holy Spirit, and born to a young virgin girl named Mary. The purpose of His life on earth was to die for humanity, which He did in a magnificent and gloriously painful way. In His death and resurrection, He provided the way for the forgiveness of our sins and opened the way for us to commune with Him all the days of our lives. He gives healing for sickness and comforts us in times of great sorrow. His love is like no earthly love you will ever experience; it is complete, fulfilling, life-changing, and powerful. The Bible says that "God so loved the world, that He gave His only begotten Son [Jesus Christ] so that whosoever would believe in Him, would have eternal life" (John 3:16 KJV).

If you would like to receive Jesus Christ as your personal Savior, it is as easy as admitting that you have hurt others and you are a sinner. Then, confess that you are sorry for your wrongdoings. We have all done, thought, or said things that the Bible calls sin. "All have sinned and fall short of the glory of God" (Romans 3:23 KJV).

The book of Romans continues, "For the wages of sin is death, but the free gift of God [that is, His remarkable, overwhelming gift of grace to believers] is eternal life in Christ Jesus our Lord" (Romans 6:23 AMP).

Jesus died in our place so that we could have a relationship with God and live with Him eternally.

"God demonstrates his own love toward us, in that while we were yet sinners, Christ died for us" (Romans 5:8 NKJV).

We are told that Jesus is the only way to God. "I am the way, the truth and the life; no one comes to the Father, except through me" (John 14:6 NKJV).

You cannot earn your salvation, and no amount of good works will qualify you. We are saved by God's grace when we have faith in Jesus Christ, His Son. Our part is to believe this as the truth.

Can you admit that you are a sinner?

Can you accept that Jesus died for your sins?

Can you ask Him to forgive you?

Then, I would encourage you to turn from your sins and allow Jesus Christ to love you. What matters to Him is the attitude of your heart. Be honest and open with Him and hold nothing back. I promise you He can handle it!

Pray

Dear God, I know I am a sinner, and I ask for Your forgiveness. I believe that Jesus Christ is Your Son. I believe that He died for my sins and that You raised Him to life. I want to trust Him as my Savior and follow Him as Lord from this day forward. Guide my life and help me to do Your will. I pray this in the name of Jesus Christ. Amen.

Jared's Story

When I found out that my dad had cancer, I was in Vancouver. I had finished my shift at Sneaker Box (a sneaker retail store). My mother called me and told me she had some news for me. She could only tell me the information if I was sitting. I was in a bit of a rush since I was headed out to take a dance class, but regardless, I listened to her and sat down. I didn't know how to react when I heard he was diagnosed with leukemia. It felt like life had somehow betrayed me. I wanted it to be a lie or a joke so bad. But I knew it wasn't. I was quiet and held it together. I was trying to be strong for my mother on the phone while believing we would work through it. I didn't break down until I called my girlfriend to tell her the information I had just received. Once you say something, it makes it real and carries a lot of weight, and I couldn't even finish the sentence. I don't remember what was said. All I remember is that moment's emotions, the location, and some minor details.

I broke down in the middle of a park, crying. It's one of those things that, as a kid, you believed would never happen to you or your parents. They are supposed to grow old and be at your wedding and watch you maneuver through life. They would meet your kids and give you life advice. It felt like everything had been interrupted. Nothing was for sure at this point, but it all just flooded over me.

A part of me felt selfish to have been in Vancouver chasing my dream as an actor and dancer, and I wasn't there to be beside my dad while going through the largest battle of his life. My father, however, always corrected me. He wanted nothing more for me than to chase my dream and not let his illness get in the way. I was always very positive through it all and had a firm belief he would fight through and be all right. I didn't deny that death was a genuine possibility, but my father always taught me to focus on the good in everything while also being aware of all possible outcomes.

During my dad's illness, I was fortunate to have some solid support systems, these being my girlfriend, best friend, mother, and even my dad. My girlfriend was the most unique as I would have complete meltdowns with her, and she did a tremendous job helping me even though she didn't know what to do or say. Her listening always helped. I had many self-doubts and felt so guilty being here in Vancouver and not with my dad.

One of the most important things that helped me through this was letting the emotions flow and not holding anything back. If I felt sad and needed to cry, I would just cry and accept that's what I needed at that moment. I would also have moments where I would get frustrated that this was happening to my father and my family and how unfair it was. Although those feelings were valid, I needed to accept everything for what it was and not ignore it. Talking to my mom was always helpful. She was going through the same thing. But it was also different as this was my father. It was her best friend, partner, and soulmate.

Watching my mother go through all this pain sucked. My parents truly loved each other like no one I've ever seen. It was truly genuine love. My father loved my mother and his family so much. He always wanted what was best for us and sacrificed his time and money to live the life he wanted us to. Having conversations with him while he was sick was, oddly, such a blessing. He always wanted to hear about me, how I was doing in Vancouver, and about the shows and movies I was working on. Watching him go through this and having him say goodbye to us was heartbreaking. He honestly loved us more than anything in the world.

During the last few moments of his life, I was so fortunate to have been in Edmonton visiting him and my family when we had to take him to the hospital and found out he had a brain bleed. I was right beside him, holding his hand. It hurt so much, but I'm so happy I got to spend his last few days at home with him and enjoy some laughs and our final good times. While he was in the hospital in palliative care, I had to go back home to work, but I got to have my last goodbye.

A few days after I returned to Vancouver, I got a call from my mother that my father had passed away. I didn't sleep that night; I just cried. That's all I could do: cry. Everything felt surreal and yet so real. It felt like life would be incomplete without him, and yet I had to just continue with life like nothing happened, even though my whole life had just been forever altered. It felt like no one cared.

I don't know what I expected anyone to do or say. Everything people said felt annoying but also appreciated. People would try to make it better, even though there is no way to make it better. I had people try to relate to it, even though they had never experienced death or loss, telling me they could pull some parallels because their dad is blind or ill. Obviously, everyone has their battles, but nothing can relate to losing a parent. A few of my friends had also lost their parents because of illness, and I found a lot of healing and good support through them.

When comforting someone who is dealing with loss, don't try to suggest anything. Don't try to relate. Just send your love and support and listen if they want to talk about it. At the end of the day, this is their journey and theirs alone, and they will find a way through it with or without you. It's not your place to give input unless they ask you. "Sorry for your loss" was probably one of the most annoying responses only because you'd hear it so much. Still, it always felt genuine as they genuinely didn't know what to say and didn't try to make it better or say something silly and out of place.

I appreciated all the love and support I got, regardless of some of the hurtful things people would say. Everyone has their way of grieving and dealing with things, but as long as they're dealing with them, it's good. I learned from the best: my father. He was a big softy. He was good at showing his emotion and encouraging my brother and me, as kids, that crying and allowing yourself to feel these emotions were OK. It was healthy to face them straight on, not hiding them or bottling them up. My dad also would make jokes about hardships or tough times, always finding light in a dark circumstance, which I also find myself doing. I make dead-dad jokes when I feel the time is appropriate with the right people. By doing that, I'm recognizing my pain's existence and moving through it. I still have the days when I cry and break down because I miss him or have something I want to tell or ask him. I just allow myself to go through it. Sitting in the pain and recognizing its effect on your life makes you much stronger and heals you.

Through my experience, I have learned a lot and now have a new outlook on life. Cherish every moment with everyone you love. You never know when you won't see them again. Never go to bed mad at someone or something. Life is more significant than that, and it's never worth the energy to hold on to something that makes you angry. Everyone has their battles, and you never know if they're having a rough day, so be friendly and patient with them and yourself.

I don't have the answer to anyone going through something similar and looking for advice on how to act or what to do. All I can say is take it day by day and allow yourself to feel how you feel—it's natural. Be patient with yourself. You're on a journey, and it's not an easy one. It's one that takes a lot of time and effort. There will be days when you just feel exhausted, and your brain doesn't quite work correctly. It can be very frustrating at times but allow yourself to be there and be present. No amount of anger, jealousy, or spite will bring my dad back. All I can do is be thankful for the life I had with him and everything he taught me. I miss him, and I always will, and I will always have days when I break into tears and say I miss him. It will never get easier without him, but knowing this helps you better understand yourself and how to deal with it.

Jared Outten

Joel's Story

When my dad was diagnosed, I don't remember much. I do remember dreading the battle to come but never doubting for an instant that he would make it through. After all, that's how we were raised.

"Look at all possible outcomes. Focus on the worst-case scenario. 'Can you live with that?'" he would ask every time. When we finally said yes, he would tell us, "Now run for the best! You already know the worst-case scenario and are OK with it. What do you have to lose?"

WHAT NOT TO SAY

I understood that my dad could die, but he was Dad and only fifty years young, plus God was on our side. Surely, this battle was already won. Needless to say, I was not prepared for the battle to come. As time continued, I became more cognizant of the perilous journey we were on. I watched Dad deteriorate—and I mean exactly that. As time pressed on, he became less dad as I knew him and more this sick dad that I could hardly recognize. Don't get me wrong. He was still my father, the very man who held every answer to life's questions that a young man would have, but he no longer looked invincible.

My wife and I moved out of our townhouse and into Mom and Dad's to help with Dad and to be close to him. At this point, Dad was always tired because of the chemo. He often didn't feel good or hungry. This is when he started to become thinner. I remember people would say, "Your dad is young and healthy. He is going to beat this," "Have faith for healing," and "I'm sorry you, guys, are going through this at a young age." This was still early in the timeline, and honestly, I took most advice as helpful and hopeful.

As time went on and Dad continued to worsen, we realized we were in dire straits. I noticed my faith being stretched to new levels. But there was still a chance! We were sent to see a bone marrow specialist in a city three hours from home. At this point, we were told that without a bone marrow transplant, Dad was terminal, but the doctors at home were hopeful and in good spirits that Dad would be accepted for the transplant. When we got to Calgary and arrived at the hospital, time slowed down. Every step was heavy with dread. This was the last line. Depending on this specialist, Dad lived or died. The noise became muffled as I walked around the hospital. It's as if I were a victim of a nearby grenade, like in a war movie. I am not sure how long the whole thing lasted, but eventually, we were taken into a large conference room where we sat down. Everyone was quiet, but there was the odd joke to lighten the tension.

At last, the doctor came in, sat on the other side of the table, and time stopped. This was it. What was he going to say? The words echoed inside my brain for the longest second of my life: "The surgery would be higher risk than the cancer. We will not be doing the transplant."

I had been shot. I remember very little of the moments in the room after that, except this: my wife was yelling at the doctor, processing things differently as she does. My mother, father, and I quietly processed what his statement meant. The cancer was a death sentence at this point, and surgery would be worse? And my uncle, who was there for support, just uttered, "Well, that just really stinks." The drive home was silent—a few jokes and tears—but mostly silence.

Not long after that meeting, Dad went into remission. We were happy. We celebrated. We cheered for about three months. Then, he began to present symptoms again. This time, it was more aggressive, faster, and harder to deal with. It was that summer my wife told me she was pregnant; I could not wait to tell my parents! I took the rest of the day off with my wife, and we went and bought "Grandma" and "Grandpa" coffee mugs. We took them home and presented them to my mom and dad as quickly as possible. Mom threw her hands up in the air with joy, and Dad stared at the cup for a moment before starting to cry. He was so emotional; he gave me a big hug, said congratulations, and then went to his room for a while. We talked periodically about fatherhood and what was to come.

A couple of months later, I was at work. I had only been there about a month. My mom called, "You need to get off work. Your dad has a brain bleed, and he doesn't have long." I left work that day with the surrounding world slowed and muffled, exactly like the day at the specialist. I walked in and saw my mom and my brother standing over Dad. His words were slurred and hard to piece together. He was definitely at the end now. We visited every day after work and brought him snacks and drinks. This one time, my wife and I brought a booster juice, and we let Dad have a little. We thought he was nearly comatose, but he sat straight up out of bed and reached to have more. Of course, we gave him the cup! Dad was always about not interrupting anything and trying to make the most out of every situation, so it was no surprise that he held to the following Friday to ensure everyone got one more work week in. But, alas, it was done. He was at peace.

Through this experience, I would point out that I felt most supported when people would just listen, let me tell stories about Dad, and joke with me about memories that they might have of him. Some advice about our relationship that I got while he was still alive that was so good:

"Talk to him."

"Tell him how you feel."

"Don't let anything you regret be unsaid."

On the other hand, I felt brushed off when people would say the cliché without asking any questions, "He is going to be OK. He is still young and has lots to fight for." Sometimes, people would just walk away. This was not helpful. I understand listening can be uncomfortable, but at least listen to the conversation or tell me something, like, "I don't know how to respond." Walking away makes the person who is grieving or hurt feel like a burden.

During the grieving process, I felt lost. My son was five months away, and now *my* dad was gone. I remember thinking everything I would need from my father would have to come from memory. I will get no fatherly advice from him, who I would like it from the most. I will not know the things he "would have done differently."

I was hugely blessed to have had my employers at that time. They were incredibly supportive as they did know my dad quite well. After he passed, they told me to take my time and grieve and then surprised me with a full paycheck.

For *What Not to Say*, I would break this into two parts:

1. First, when someone is sick, don't say stuff without thinking. Practice empathy. Ask yourself the question, "How would I feel

if that was said to me?" For example, don't say, "I had a dream. Your father was at your son's fifth birthday, so I believe he will be well, and he still has a long life." That makes me feel great until he's dead. Now, I'm thinking of all the things I clung to, like my son's fifth birthday. Don't say anything as an absolute. I understand the want to comfort, but honestly, the best way is to ask questions. Don't give unsolicited advice; it is seriously unhelpful. At the end of a conversation, maybe say, "Hey, give me a call if you want to chat." Then, be available for the chat.

2. Second, what not to say after passing: The hardest thing to hear from someone—and this goes for both during and after the sickness—is "I know how you feel." The more emphasis you put on this, the less caring you sound. The truth is, you don't have any idea! I heard this one so many times, and it was always followed by a story of exactly how they don't. One person said this after Dad passed and then told me how their estranged mother survived bone cancer—totally not helpful. First, I was close to my dad. Second, he had acute myeloid leukemia. Third—and this one is the kicker—*he died*!

Moving forward, I would tell anyone going through this that watching a loved one go through sickness is hard and will never get easier; it just becomes more "normal." You will get through this. There will be tears. There will be smiles and laughs. There will be times when you hurt so bad you drop to your knees and bawl your eyes out! This is normal. Don't let anyone tell you otherwise. You're not weak, and you're not fragile. You're hurt in an inexplicable way, and your soul is going to find some way to let it out. Find someone you trust and who will listen to you, and I don't mean listen to a bit and then tell you what they think. I don't mean someone who is going to try to fix it. I mean someone who will listen to the whole thing even if you start crying and then just hug and comfort you. Ignore the goofy things people are going to say. They want to help; they just don't know how, so take it as that. They are offering assuage. Lastly, you will get through this. It is going to suck a lot, and at times, you will want to hide away and let the world pass by. That is fine, but don't stay there. Come out as soon as possible. Although it may not look like it, your loved ones are also gathering strength from watching you fight.

Remember

You are safer in the storm if that is where you are meant to be than keeping yourself safe.

Joel Outten

Epilogue

The Dream
September 9, 2015

The Dream: Part 1

In the dream, I was driving down Center Street in Calgary, Alberta, Canada. I was heading east toward the overpass onto Stony Trail north toward Edmonton, Alberta. I was unsure of what I was doing in Calgary, but it didn't feel like I was there for something pleasant. There was a feeling of pressure and emptiness inside of me as I drove.

As I approached the overpass, I waited for the light to turn green. When it did, I did a quick check in both directions to ensure no one was running the red light and proceeded into the turn. I had seen no traffic, yet to my surprise, I was T-boned so hard by a fast-moving vehicle that it catapulted me off the bridge and over the side down to the road below.

As I went over the bridge, I could see a huge angel standing between heaven and earth, and he put his hand underneath our van and placed it gently down on the number one highway. I got out of my vehicle, shaken but unharmed. I walked to the front of the van and looked back up at the bridge. I could see a man standing there looking over at me and declaring, "It's a miracle, it's a miracle, it's a miracle!"

The Dream: Part 2

It seemed as if the curtain was dropped and then pulled up again, like at a live theater production, and I found myself in the second part of the dream. I was now in a hospital, walking down a corridor. The color on the walls was a very pale yellow, hospital yellow, and some of the walls were hospital green. I was then in a room. The walls were off-white, and I was aware that there were two beds in the room, with a curtain pulled between the two. I was standing by the bed next to the window, and from that vantage point, I could see the STARS air ambulance landing pad.

I could see a food tray on the table and some drinks. I also "knew" that help was needed in the shower as well as to go to the bathroom, but I was unsure who needed help. There was a table to the side of the bathroom with papers and a pen, and I knew that was for me. The nurses' station was directly across from the room door, where I could see cabinets, files, and drawers full of what was needed to care for the patients properly.

In the dream, I remember wondering why I was in the hospital and who needed help showering if I had been uninjured when I was T-boned. And then I wondered why on earth I would be required to write things down if I was so ill, injured, or otherwise incapacitated.

In the corner of my room, I could see that water was beginning to trickle down from the top corners, causing the room and halls to become larger. Even in the dream, I understood that this would mean an expansion of faith.

The Dream: Part 3

Like a swoosh, I found myself suddenly thrust into my home, which somehow looked very much the same yet very different, almost like it was my "new home"? I was so exhausted in the dream. I was so much more tired than I have ever been in my life—bone weary, really. I sat down heavily in a chair facing toward my kitchen while my sons, Joel and Jared, were to the left of me, sitting together on a sofa. They were looking at me. My pastor and his wife were sitting close and opposite me, also looking at me. James was not beside me. I could see him sitting far, far away. He had something on his face, like a blue mask, but I could see him smiling. His legs were crossed. He wore khaki capris, a white-and-blue checked shirt, and his favorite hat. But he was so far away it seemed he wasn't even in the house.

From there, I looked up to the end of the top cupboard, and on it was a calendar. I cannot remember the picture on it, but I did see the numbered part. I could make out that the month I was looking at began with *Ma*, but I couldn't tell if it was March or May. I could see that the year was 2016. Also circled in red was the last day of the month before the blank spot at the end of the month. To clarify, it was May 25, 2016. Below that were many lily pads that made a kind of garden path, not linear but with high and low points; below that, written in bold red capital letters and underlined three times, were the words "WRITE YOUR BOOK!"

Understanding of the Dream: Part 1

It was at the Foothills Hospital in Calgary where we met the transplant doctor. He told us that there was nothing he could do, meaning he couldn't do the transplant. This was due to a few things: the bone marrow donor was not a perfect match, there was some heart damage because of a heart attack he had suffered fifteen months previously, and he had kidney damage that occurred when he was first diagnosed with AML and admitted to hospital from a severe infection during the initial round of chemotherapy. We were told all this in the bluntest of ways.

I can still hear the doctor's voice, "I can still do the transplant if you want. You will be very sick, and you will die. All this will take three weeks, and you will die without family by your side. Is that what you want? Or do you want to go home and live the next three months of your life enjoying your family and friends?" We were definitely hit hard! That incident in Calgary permanently changed the direction of my life and coincided with the part in the dream where I was T-boned and thrown off the bridge.

I believe the angel represents the divine protection, provision, purposes, and intervention of God we experienced so much while we were in the midst of his illness. The man on the bridge said "It's a miracle" three times. My husband should have died within the first week of discovering he had AML, but he did not. He should never have lived fifteen months, but he did. He should never have gone into remission, but he did. The added bonus was that in all the months of his illness, he never experienced any pain whatsoever until he had the brain bleed, although he felt nauseated every day to some degree. Of course, other "miracles" happened during the fifteen months, but I won't cover them all here.

Understanding of the Dream: Part 2

The hospital corridors I walked down in the University of Alberta Hospital and one of the rooms where I stood in the dream were the very corridors and one of the rooms he was in. The colors were exact, and the bed looking out to the landing pad of STARS air ambulance was the same. James was so sick initially that he needed assistance with some of the simplest of tasks, most especially showering. That room faced the nurses' station and the trolleys filled with all the nursing equipment. Beside that trolley were the files, just as I had seen them.

The table with pens and paper was for me for the notes I would take (unknowingly) for this book. The expansion of faith that I saw in the room and corridors was happening in a genuine way for us. Hanging on to faith in the middle of a storm made our faith grow enormously.

Understanding of the Dream: Part 3

True to the dream, I was more exhausted than I had ever been in my life when I came home the morning my husband died. I was sure I had never experienced exhaustion like that, and I felt it for weeks afterward. I understood the meaning of my husband being so far removed from me, as well as my sons and my pastors looking at me. What was I going to do now? I needed them to be there, walk, sit, and be with me! And on many occasions in the summer months during his illness, my husband wore the same clothes I had seen in the dream. I never said a word to him about any of it.

The calendar was correct down to the date of the day he became ill, which was May 25, 2016. It was days after my birthday outing when he thought he had gotten food poisoning. The lily pads were the many things I needed to do and go through before I could begin to write this book. There can be much to do after a person passes, and then there is the healing process. While much of the tedious paper filing has a timeline in which it needs to be completed, the healing process does not.

I knew I had come to the place and time to take my writing seriously when I went to a conference. While I was there, the person praying told me I was to "write a book." This person had no prior knowledge of my story or the dream I had over two years before. At this conference, I also met the individual who helped put the puzzle pieces together on paper to create what would become this book.

When God speaks, He accomplishes that which He has spoken. I admit I may not have enjoyed the entire journey, but I am so very thankful He is in control.

What Not to Say

I wrote this book from the only point of view I have, which is one of illness and death. I recognize that many areas of loss are not covered in these pages. I tried to draw many of those things into the dialogue, but I want you to understand that the truths contained in this book could and should be recognized in different kinds of loss. Many of the principles are easily transferable and should be applied in most, if not all, situations. I sincerely hope this book helps you transition from struggling to cope with what has been said to you to knowing how to respond in kindness. For those wanting to be a helpful shoulder to lean on and support for your aching friend but feel like you keep making things worse, be encouraged. You showed up in their time of crisis, and you can do this!

In my attempt to shine a much-needed light on this subject, I summarize by saying we are never better off pretending we are not in pain, even if it is more socially acceptable. However, when I think about it, I am unsure how others would handle it if we responded honestly when asked the question, "How are you?" But then again, would we even ask the question if we knew it would evoke an honest answer? Have we fostered a culture of "acceptability" rather than honesty, where telling a "little white lie" is better than being vulnerable and raw? This statement speaks volumes to my heart.

Shining the light on becoming more honest with ourselves was, at least, part of the goal of this book. There is no shame in hurting because someone or something you loved was stolen from you. Likewise, there should be no shame in struggling through an impending loss or health issue. What it means if you do this is that you love deeply, and that kind of love should be supported, not shunned. The lives of those around us should be celebrated while they are among us just as much as they should be after they are gone. Love does not end when the last breath is taken; it continues with every breath and heartbeat of those left behind. Love does not die!

I wanted to look at this incredibly complex topic and take the top off it in a way that makes it possible to start talking openly about it. We can do better for the hurting in the future than we have in the past. We can love better than we have loved if we stop telling others how to feel when they are in pain and stop demeaning and devaluing their grieving process. I believe it is time to "mourn with those who mourn, weep with those who weep, and rejoice with those who rejoice." There is indeed a time for everything under the sun, and while we keep that in mind, may we remember that we will likely walk the same valley sometime in our future.

You have heard me repeatedly talk about the importance of "listen to hear, not to respond." If you take anything away from this reading, I would be happy if this was it because this truth goes far beyond this topic. Many councilors, advisers, aides, and support people are available for struggling people. These people are qualified to help in areas of crisis and concern, so let's release ourselves from the responsibility of fixing those things we do not have to! Understanding that we are not responsible for healing someone else's brokenness should free us up to sit with them in their difficult moments and listen and love them just as they are. It's their moment!

I also understand that doing things the way I have suggested may require learning or relearning some things while simultaneously unlearning and discarding others. Yes, I am talking about changing how we interact with one another while also changing how we think and behave. Relearning things like showing compassion, empathy, and selflessness with the ability to have an open ear is necessary if we are going to bring acceptance and healing to those in pain.

The message from the masses is loud and clear: they are tired of being overlooked, rejected, and bullied into a way of life that they do not know how to fit into. We should be listening for this sound coming from many who mourn around us. Although we may disagree with some things, the underlying cry is the same. The people around us are hungry for love and acceptance! Our words and actions can either heal the heart like bandages and oil or wound it like a swift upper-right hook.

There is an old saying: "People don't care how much you know until they know how much you care." This saying has a lot of truth, especially regarding the things that affect our lives and hearts. Listening to the overall message those around us are living is always good because hearing their hearts' needs will help us understand how to fill the demand. The message is loud and clear! And the message is this: the hurting doesn't care how much money we have, the letters behind our names, or how many followers we have on our social media profiles. What they want to know, and what they ask without words, is this: "Can you love me for me? Can you love me in my sin? Love me in my pain? Love me in my confusion? Love me for me?"

Before We Part

Perhaps you have read this far and find yourself thrust into a situation where you have a friend going through drastic life changes, and loss and grief wallop them. You want to know how to begin to step up but need help figuring out what to do first. Here are three quick, easy, helpful suggestions for those who want to be fully present and available.

Listen to Hear, Not to Respond

Bring the coffee, the donuts, or lunch, and settle down when you are open and available to listen and ask questions. It is vital that you honor them and their pain, so making sure you are not distracted or having to rush off shows your level of care. Ask them to tell their story if they want to and if they are able to and don't offer advice. Please let them dictate the amount they want to share and how they want to share it. Remember, you do not need to fix them or their problem; just let them share their heart. Always remember it is OK to weep with them.

Offer Assistance in Areas Where You Know You Can and Will Help. Then Do It!

We all want to help, and there is no time when it is more needed than during a loss, but make sure the offer comes with the doing. Be the hands and feet that mow the lawn, weed the garden, bale the hay, cook the meals, do the childcare, drive to appointments, or help to take out the trash. Be quick to respond when the offer is accepted and be willing to do it more than once because their situation and grief will take much longer than a few short weeks to heal. Plan to be available instead of trying to fit it into an already-tight schedule and let them know which day(s) you will be able to help.

Help Them Feel Like They Are Doing It Right

As you walk through their journey, a big key is helping them see what they are doing right. People under challenging circumstances have so much going on that they can easily become overwhelmed, feel inadequate and frustrated, or believe they are making all the mistakes. So many voices are coming their way that steal their confidence, courage, and strength. Be the *other* voice! Be the one who encourages, uplifts, and celebrates their decisions, even when you disagree. Remember, this is not your journey, and they are not your decisions to make, but your friend will need your support, regardless.

As I close, let me encourage you to consider another old saying when you wonder if what you want to do is right. Ask yourself these questions:

Is it helpful?

Is it kind?

Is it necessary?

May God bless you abundantly as you move forward in love and grace to help those who need you during their most vulnerable and painful times.

Love does not end the moment the last breath is taken.

It continues with every breath and heartbeat of those left behind!

Love does not die.

The greatest of these is *love* (1 Corinthians 13:13)!

Cheryl Outten-Bay